THE ARMCHAIR OLYMPIAN

Phil Ascough

BLOOMSBURY

First published in Great Britain 2012

Copyright © 2012 by Phil Ascough

The moral right of the author has been asserted

Bloomsbury Publishing Plc
50 Bedford Square
London WC1B 3DP

www.bloomsbury.com

Bloomsbury Publishing, London, New York, Berlin and Sydney

A CIP catalogue record for this book is available from the British Library

ISBN 978-1-408-16476-1

10 9 8 7 6 5 4 3 2 1

Designed and typeset in Great Britain by Cox and Wyman, Reading, UK

CONTENTS

INTRODUCTION:
Are You Sitting Comfortably?

When Spyridon Louis won the marathon at the first modern Olympics in 1896, his gift from the king was a horse and cart. They were to help Louis in his day job of transporting barrels of fresh water twice a day to sell to the people of Athens.

Fast-forward 100 years. There's no way Josiah Thugwane would have been allowed within marathon distance of the Olympic venue with any beverage other than official sponsor-fizz. By the time of the Atlanta Games, corporate was king.

The cost of hosting the Games makes such involvement essential of course, with huge sums returned from sponsorship and from media rights. And competition to secure those deals and then to protect the benefits is as fierce as anything on the track or in the pool.

It doesn't necessarily follow that the 21st-century Olympic Games are any less worthy than the 20th-century version or even the one edition held in the 19th century. Examples of sharp practice are not confined to the modern era, they just reach a wider audience.

And it is interesting to consider what the modern media might have made of some of the stars and scoundrels of Games gone by. Would they pay more for a stairlift promo by Oscar Swahn, a shooting medallist at 72, or a mobile phone clip of Fred Lorz, hopping in and out of a car during the 1904 marathon?

This book remembers some of the all-time greats across the ages of the modern Games – the winners and the losers, the champions and the cheats. It draws on records and anecdotes from a number of sources, some first-hand, some reported, some obviously reliable and some a bit dubious but too entertaining to leave out.

And it's called *The Armchair Olympian* because, realistically, that's as close as most of us are going to get to the action.

FIRSTS

The spirit of innovation has been one of the driving forces behind the development of the Games, even if on occasions the Olympic vision has proved to be a little blurred.

Sports are introduced, demonstrated, discarded and occasionally restored depending on the prevailing culture of the host city and people. Old traditions have been preserved and in some cases brought up to date using technology which has also taken the organisation of the Games to new levels. And women have been first ignored, then accommodated and finally encouraged.

The awarding of gold, silver and bronze medals for the first three places was not introduced until 1904, and has since been backdated to recognise achievements in the first two editions of the Games. Many participants have also benefited from the efforts to reduce the duration of the Games to a couple of weeks rather than several months, from the move to admit professional performers and from the accompanying astronomical increases in revenue and audience reach from sponsorship and TV.

There have been changes to customs and ceremonies, to infrastructure and equipment, to the security of athletes, spectators and venues. And, with depressing but necessary frequency, to the investigation and detection of cheats.

More nations, more people and more money all combine to make the Olympic Games bigger and bigger. But – uniquely for a major sporting event – the Games retain their values and the changes are almost always for the better, not least for the doves.

20/12 Challenges

Warm-up Stretches

The founder of the Olympic movement, Baron Pierre de Coubertin, was also the first Secretary General of the International Olympic Committee. He became its President in 1896.

The first event of the modern Olympics was a heat of the 100m won by the American runner Francis Lane, who later finished third in the final. The first gold medal was won by another American, James Connolly, in what was then known as the hop, step and jump.

Women were allowed to compete in selected events at the Olympics in 1900. They took part in swimming events from 1912 and were admitted to track and field events from 1928.

Hélène de Pourtalès was the first woman to win Olympic gold. She was part of the Swiss crew that won the 1–2 ton sailing class in 1900. Charlotte Cooper of Great Britain was the first to win an individual Olympic event in the 1900 tennis tournament, in which she also won the mixed doubles.

India made their first appearance at the Games in 1900 and later dominated the hockey tournament. But the nation had to wait more than 100 years for a first individual gold. It came when Abhinav Bindra won the men's 10m air rifle competition in 2008.

"The most important thing in the Olympic Games is not to win but to take part, just as the most important thing in life is not the triumph but the struggle. The essential thing is not to have conquered but to have fought well."

The Olympic creed, based on a speech at the 1908 Games by Bishop Ethelbert Talbot

The Olympic Oath and the Olympic flag were first introduced at the 1920 Games in Antwerp, as was the release of doves to symbolise peace.

Dublin-born John Boland won tennis gold in singles and doubles under the Great Britain flag at the 1896 Games. Ireland made its first Games appearance in its own right at the Paris Olympics in 1924.

Brunei made its first appearance at the Olympic Games in 1988, sending one official and no competitors. The south-east Asian country sent one athlete to each Games in 1996, 2000 and 2004 but was excluded in 2008 for failing to register any athletes.

Drug-testing for all sports was introduced to the Olympic Games in 1968, first at the winter event in Grenoble and then at the summer Games in Mexico City.

Anni Holdmann of Germany became the first woman to win a track and field event when she took first place in a heat of the 100m in 1928. Poland's Halina Konopacka was the first woman to win a gold when she triumphed in the 1928 discus.

Innovations at Stockholm in 1912 included the use of photo-finish in some track events and – following the introduction of the opening parade at London in 1908 – the practice of an athlete carrying a sign bearing their nation's name.

The first torch relay for a summer Games took place as part of the build-up to the Berlin Olympics in 1936. A total of 3,331 runners carried the torch from the Temple of Zeus in Olympia through seven countries in all to the stadium.

Berlin was also the first Games to be televised, albeit only to communal viewing rooms. In 1948 the broadcast could be viewed by people within range of Wembley and during the 1960s coverage became more widespread, with live pictures transmitted around the world.

Figure skating was the first winter sport to feature in an edition of the summer Games when it was added to the schedule for London in 1908. Ice hockey was contested in 1920 but winter sports were given their own Games four years later.

Christa Luding-Rothenburger made history in 1988 by becoming the first person to win medals in the summer and winter Games in the same year. The East German had won speed skating gold and silver earlier in the year and followed up with a cycling silver in Seoul.

The Los Angeles Olympics in 1932 had an unofficial mascot and the Mexico edition had a red jaguar with no name, but the first official named mascot of the summer Games came in 1972 with a dachshund called Waldi.

The IOC's revenue from worldwide TV deals exceeded $1billion for the first time at the 2000 Games in Sydney. For Beijing it was close to $1.8billion with sponsorship worth an additional $1.2billion.

The construction of a swimming tank within the White City stadium track in 1908 meant that for the first time Olympic aquatic events did not take place in open water.

Hockey was played on an artificial surface for the first time at the Olympics in 1976. New Zealand beat Australia 1–0 in the final in Montreal.

The Olympic motto of "Citius, Altius, Fortius" – Swifter, Higher, Stronger – was first used in the opening ceremony for the 1924 summer Games in Paris.

Race For The Line

1 *What went on sale to the public in April 1896 to help raise funds for the first Games?*

2 *What sort of animal was Misha, the mascot for the 1980 Games in Moscow?*

3 *Which team won the ice hockey event in 1920, the only time the sport featured in the summer Games schedule?*

4 *Only five nations have been present at every summer Olympics: Greece, Great Britain, France, Australia and which other?*

5 *What was used in sprint races for the first time in an Olympics at London in 1948?*

6 *At which Games were several doves of peace burned alive as the Olympic flame was ignited, prompting a re-think for the next Games?*

7 *What were the live targets that were used in the Olympic shooting programme for the first and last time in Paris in 1900?*

8 *Apart from sailing, which is the only Olympic sport in which men and women compete together?*

9 *Which Games were the first to be hit by a political boycott against a background of the Hungarian Revolution, the Suez Crisis and tensions in China?*

10 *Which combat sport contested at every modern Games except one was added to the women's programme for the first time at London 2012?*

"I am extremely delighted that you have realised the dream of a billion people."

Indian President Prathiba Patil after Abhinav Bindra won the nation's first individual Olympic gold

11 *In which event did IOC President Jacques Rogge compete for the first time in Mexico in 1968?*

12 *Which country leads the opening parade of nations as part of a tradition which began in Amsterdam in 1928?*

Answers:

1 Commemorative stamps
2 A bear
3 Canada
4 Switzerland
5 Starting blocks
6 Seoul
7 Pigeons
8 Equestrian
9 Melbourne in 1956
10 Boxing
11 Sailing
12 Greece

CITIES AND VENUES

Controversy – and there has been plenty of it – is covered elsewhere, but it doesn't get any bigger than two World Wars and other international conflicts which scarred the first half of the 20th century.

Add to that the problems created by petty politics, post-war rationing and the odd volcano erupting and it's a wonder the Olympic Games ever get staged at all.

Transport on an Olympic scale is tricky enough in this day and age, and was no doubt a factor all those years ago behind keeping the Games in Europe between 1904 and 1932. That said, a schedule of Belgium in 1920, France in 1924 and the Netherlands in 1928 hardly underlined ambitions of global expansion.

Post-war poverty was evident in 1948, with reports that the Dutch delivered 100 tons of fruit to London for the Olympics, with the Danes contributing 160,000 eggs. Given that scenario, coupled with London's late emergence as a rescue venue in 1908 and the cash squeeze in the build-up to 2012, it's fair to wonder what the city might produce given some time to plan and a bit of cash to spend.

History shows that economic difficulties are a fact of Olympic life – but that, even with Los Angeles and the rest of the United States in the grip of the Great Depression, the French got their priorities spot-on.

17

20/12 Challenges

Warm-up Stretches

"Hopefully the Olympic Games will expose more people to the reality of life in China. The Olympic Games will be some kind of vehicle to showcase China's opening up to the world."

Wang Wei, Secretary General of the Beijing Organising Committee

London became the first city to be selected to host a third full edition of the summer Games when it won the bidding process in 2005. London's first Games was in 1908 and the city hosted the event again in 1948.

Amsterdam applied to host the Games three times before finally winning selection. The Dutch were unsuccessful candidates in 1916, 1920 and 1924 but welcomed representatives of 46 countries in 1928.

The Hungarian capital, Budapest, was placed on stand-by when concerns emerged about whether the facilities in Athens would be ready in time – for the first Olympic Games of the modern era in 1896.

The 1916 Games in Berlin were cancelled following the outbreak of the First World War. Germany welcomed the world as Olympic Games host in 1936 – the last Games before the outbreak of the Second World War.

Rio de Janeiro became the first South American city to win selection to host the Games. The venue for 2016 overcame Madrid by 66 votes to 32 in the final round of voting, having trailed the Spanish capital in the first ballot.

Chicago, which reached the final four candidates in the race to host 2016, was selected to host the 1904 event. But controversially the Games were moved from the Windy City to St Louis to coincide with the World's Fair organised to celebrate the purchase of Louisiana from France.

The 1940 Games were moved from Tokyo to Helsinki after the outbreak of war between the proposed hosts and China. They were postponed to 1944 after the outbreak of the Second World War and they finally took place in 1948. In London.

The three editions of the Games to have been cancelled are still included in the numbering. Berlin in 1916 was VI, Helsinki in 1940 was XII and London in 1944 was XIII.

The 1906 Games in Athens, often called the Intercalated Games because they were inserted into the planned schedule, are not included in the numbering and are not listed in official IOC records. But they are credited by some for helping to stabilise the Games movement after the problems of Paris and St Louis.

Early editions of the Games often lasted for several months –
Paris from May to October, St Louis from July until November
and London from April until October. The more condensed
schedule was introduced from 1932 in Los Angeles.

Paris was the first city to host the summer Olympic Games
twice. The French capital has not been selected since 1924
and was a strong rival to London's bid for 2012.

Los Angeles, Minneapolis and Philadelphia each lodged bids
to host the Games for 1948, 1952 and 1956 and were joined at
various stages of the process by Baltimore, Chicago, Detroit
and San Francisco. But the Games did not return to LA and
the United States until 1984, 52 years after their previous visit.

At Atlanta in 1996 all the recognised National Olympic
Committees were represented for the first time – a total of
197. The opening ceremony was performed by Bill Clinton,
President of the United States.

The Olympic flame flew through the air from Athens to Ottawa
in 1976 – but not by plane. A sensor turned ionised particles
of the flame into coded impulses which were then transmitted
by satellite to Canada and used to activate a laser beam which
lit the torch ready for the journey to the stadium in Montreal.

Barcelona's flame ceremony of 1992 was exposed by those
who doubted the wisdom of firing a flaming arrow over the
heads of the crowd and into the cauldron. It emerged that
Antonio Rebollo had indeed been ordered to overshoot in
the interests of safety while behind-the-scenes trickery
was used to complete the stunt.

London was not even on the list of candidate cities to host the 1908 Games but stepped in at short notice to replace Rome. Money was the problem for the Italians, who had to fund the rebuilding of Naples following the eruption of Mount Vesuvius in 1906.

Altitude was a major concern after the 1968 Games were awarded to Mexico City. Competitors in endurance events encountered difficulties which were reflected in slower times than four years previously, while athletes in many throwing, jumping and sprinting categories set challenging new records.

Cricket has only featured in the Olympic Games schedule once but the Melbourne Cricket Ground was the centrepiece of the 1956 edition. The venue for more than 100 cricket Test matches, the MCG was home to athletics as well as the hockey and football finals.

The number of women participants exceeded 1,000 for the first time at Munich in 1972, but they were still outnumbered by men by nearly six to one.

Moscow submitted an unsuccessful bid for the 1976 Games but four years later became the first Communist hosts of the event, winning nearly twice as many IOC votes as Los Angeles.

Race For The Line

1 *Which South American city was an unsuccessful candidate to host the Games in 1956, 1958 and 2004?*

2 *What luxury were the French athletes given special dispensation to take to Los Angeles with them in 1932?*

3 *Which former Olympic boxing gold medallist and subsequent world heavyweight champion lit the Olympic flame at Atlanta in 1996?*

4 *Gliding was a demonstration sport in the 1936 Games, but which other aircraft flew over the stadium in Berlin in an ominous display of German military muscle?*

5 *Which European city hosted the equestrian events in 1956 when Australian quarantine regulations prevented the transport of horses to Melbourne?*

6 *What was the nickname of the Beijing National Stadium, which formed the spectacular centrepiece of the 2008 Games?*

7 *At which Games did the number of women participants exceed 4,000 for the first time?*

8 *Which Belgian city was awarded the 1920 Games in recognition of the nation's suffering during the First World War?*

9 *Which Swiss city was established as the home of the IOC in 1922?*

10 *What was presented to the IOC by the organisers of the Seoul Games in 1988 to be passed on to all future host cities?*

"With British ingenuity, wit and resourcefulness we are going to produce a Games that is going to be, in our own sweet way, just as fantastic."

Boris Johnson, Mayor of London, as the Beijing Games drew to a close

11 *Which venue hosted the tennis events at the London Games in 1908?*

12 *What was the name of the aquatics centre at the Beijing Games in 2008?*

Answers:

1 Buenos Aires
2 Wine, during the prohibition era
3 Muhammad Ali
4 The Hindenburg airship
5 Stockholm
6 The Bird's Nest
7 Sydney in 2000
8 Antwerp
9 Lausanne
10 A new Olympic flag
11 Wimbledon
12 The Water Cube

CONTROVERSIES

....

Controversies should not be confused with catastrophes and atrocities, such as the terrorist acts of Munich in 1972 and Atlanta in 1996 which demonstrated that tragedy amounts to rather more than clipping the last hurdle or falling off a bike.

Perhaps fittingly though, those attacks on the Games served to strengthen the camaraderie within the wider Olympic organisation, as indeed did the movement's defiance in the face of Adolf Hitler's grotesque posturing of 1936.

Most editions of the Games attract some controversy, usually mild but occasionally more heated. Over the years there have been concerns about Games being under-funded or over-commercialised, about there being a dearth of media coverage or a deluge, about the air being too thin or too thick.

More serious were the political boycotts which for a time threatened to become a regular part of the fabric of the Olympic Games but which haven't gained significant support since 1984.

Perhaps a greater danger to the future of the Games comes from the enemy within – the participants who seek to gain an advantage at all costs, the officials who are determined to steal the limelight, the committee members who see a bidding process as a nice little earner.

But even the most vociferous critic must admit there is usually less controversy from four years of the Olympics than from four weeks of football.

20/12 Challenge

Warm-up Stretches

The decision to compete on Sundays in the second Games in Paris in 1900 led to a bust-up between American long jump competitors Myer Prinstein and Alvin Kraenzlein. Prinstein was leading in the competition but refused to jump in the final on a Sunday – and was overhauled by one centimetre.

In 1904 the first marathon runner home was later found to have been given a lift. When the car broke down near the stadium, Fred Lorz ran all the way to the finish line. He insisted the stunt was a joke. The gold was awarded to fellow American Thomas Hicks.

Italy's Dorando Pietri headed the wrong way when he entered the stadium as leader of the 1908 marathon. Officials helped him find the finish line but he was disqualified for receiving outside aid. His genuine efforts were recognised with the presentation of a special trophy.

The 1980 Games in Moscow were boycotted by nearly 50 nations including the United States, West Germany and Japan in protest at the Soviet invasion of Afghanistan in 1979.

Jim Thorpe won the pentathlon and decathlon in 1912 in Stockholm but was stripped of his medals the following year when officials found he had once received a small amount of money to play baseball. The American's titles were reinstated but not until 1982.

"All he had was anger. After he hit me I was seeing about 48 stars. Man, oh man, I was just like a stuffed pig."

Hungarian water polo player Ervin Zádor recalls the 1956 match against the Soviet Union

Wyndham Halswelle became the first athlete to win an event with a walkover in the 1908 400m. The British runner lined up in the final with three Americans. One was disqualified for blocking him and the other two refused to compete in the re-run, which Halswelle is reported to have completed under duress.

Adolf Hitler's theories of Aryan supremacy brought calls for the United States to lead a boycott of the 1936 Games in Berlin. The Americans took part after Avery Brundage, President of the US Olympic Committee and a future IOC President, argued successfully against mixing politics and sport.

Finnish distance-running legend Paavo Nurmi was denied the chance to end his career in style when he was banned from the 1932 Games in Los Angeles. Officials decided he had breached professionalism rules by receiving excessive expenses to attend an athletics meeting in Germany.

Swedish boxer Ingemar Johansson won the world heavyweight title in 1959 but was disqualified for fleeing from Ed Sanders in the final of the 1952 Olympics boxing competition. Johansson insisted it was part of his game plan but the judges withheld his silver medal. It was reinstated in 1982.

The intense heat was blamed for the death of Danish cyclist Knud Enemark Jensen during the 100km time trial in Rome in 1960 but the later discovery that he had taken amphetamines and other substances was a factor in the IOC's move to introduce testing.

Germany, Austria, Bulgaria, Hungary and Turkey were not invited to the 1920 Games in Antwerp as a consequence of the First World War. Germany was also banned from the 1924 edition of the Games in Paris.

Rhodesia was expelled from the IOC four days before the 1972 Games in Munich as a result of protests from African nations who claimed the country was an illegal regime. It returned as Zimbabwe for the 1980 Games.

The US Olympic Committee's blunder in failing to declare Rick DeMont's medication led to the 16-year-old swimmer being disqualified for drug use after winning gold in the 400m freestyle in 1972. It took 29 years for the officials to clear DeMont's name by admitting their error.

South Africa was banned from the 1964 Games in Tokyo and later from the IOC because of the country's apartheid policies. South African athletes returned to the Games in Barcelona in 1992.

Tanzania led a boycott of the 1976 Montreal Olympics by more than 20 African countries in protest at the participation of New Zealand. The row erupted because the All Blacks had completed a rugby union tour of South Africa earlier in the year.

Political tensions surfaced when the Soviet Union and Hungary met in the water polo competition in 1956 less than two months after the Hungarian Revolution. With Hungary 4–0 up in the closing stages, the referee ended a match which he described as "a boxing match under water".

The Soviet Union reacted to the 1980 boycott by leading a revenge protest when the Games went to Los Angeles four years later. A total of 14 Soviet sympathiser nations stayed away but they had accounted for 58 per cent of the gold medals at the 1976 Games.

Tommie Smith and John Carlos came first and third respectively in the 200m at Mexico in 1968. But the two Americans were suspended and banned from the Olympic Village for giving a "Black Power" salute during the medal ceremony.

The IOC expelled 10 of its members and reviewed its bidding processes after discovering that some officials had favoured certain venues in return for bribes. The scandal focused on Salt Lake City's series of bids to host the Winter Olympics and was further fuelled by allegations of bribery around bids for summer Games.

The selection of Beijing for the 2008 Games was controversial with opponents highlighting China's human rights record and Tibetan activists calling for a boycott in protest at China's rule over their country. But the Games passed without major incident and were hailed as a success.

Race For The Line

1 *Which United States President demanded the nation's athletes boycott the Moscow Olympics in 1980?*

2 *Which South Africa-born runner competed for Great Britain in the 1984 Olympics after a newspaper campaign helped her secure British citizenship and avoid the ban on her home country?*

3 *What was blamed for the failure of American athletes to win the men's pole vault in 1972 for the first time in 66 years?*

4 *At which Games were the United States unable to field a team in the men's 4x400m relay after two of their athletes were banned for showing disrespect during the 400m medal ceremony?*

5 *Finland's athletes complained about having to compete under the flag of which nation at the 1912 Games in Stockholm?*

6 *What was the name of the athletics event organised at the University of Pennsylvania in 1980 for countries that were boycotting the Moscow Olympics?*

7 *What sort of athlete examinations were introduced by the IOC at the 1968 Olympics in Mexico City?*

8 *Which nation led a limited boycott of the 1988 Games in support of its demands to host half of the events?*

9 *Which country was barred from the 1976 Games in Montreal after insisting on competing as the Republic of China?*

> *"The political pressures in sport are becoming intolerable."*

Avery Brundage, IOC President, at the time of the expulsion of Rhodesia from the organisation

10 *Which now established Olympics sport did not feature in the schedule at Stockholm in 1912 because the Swedish organisers would not allow it?*

11 *In which event did Josia Thugwane win South Africa's first athletics gold medal after its re-admission to the Olympics in 1996?*

12 *In which event that was being contested by women for the first time did Zimbabwe win gold in their first appearance at the Games in 1980?*

Answers:

1 Jimmy Carter
2 Zola Budd
3 Their poles were banned and they were not familiar with the replacements
4 Munich 1972
5 Russia
6 The Liberty Bell Classic
7 Gender testing
8 North Korea
9 Taiwan
10 Boxing
11 The marathon
12 Hockey

HOWLERS

When it comes to something as important as the Olympic Games, preparation is everything. Years of training and sacrifice can come to nothing if performers, their coaches and even Games officials fail to expect the unexpected.

But the reality is that even perfect preparation is sometimes not quite enough. Wayward throws, dropped batons and clipped hurdles can hamper the hopes of the most experienced performers because of nerves as much as anything else.

And while performers clearly have responsibility for maintaining any kit and equipment they may need for their event, a special case has to be made for the equestrian competitors whose mounts can be rather less predictable than a bike or a boat.

Failure to keep track of the time of day – or even the dates on a calendar – is less easy to excuse, and there have been errors by athletes and officials that have resulted in medals being lost. Sometimes though, however costly a howler may appear, the athlete recovers to get back in the game.

In the case of Eric Moussambani, what appeared a disaster to the viewing millions was actually a personal best. But when it came to Paul Cerutti, even the drugs didn't work.

Warm-up Stretches

Robert Garrett of the United States was the first Olympic discus champion of the modern age with gold in 1896, when he also won the shot put. But four years later his ability deserted him as all three attempts with the discus ended out of bounds.

Farid Simaika of Egypt scored the highest points total in the men's 10m platform diving event in 1928 and was about to receive the gold medal when the judges applied additional calculations to take into account level of difficulty – and gave the gold instead to Pete Desjardins of the United States.

Marjorie Jackson of Australia won the women's 100m and 200m at Helsinki in 1952 but her team missed out on victory in the 4x100m relay when, with a comfortable lead, she dropped the baton after her hand hit a team-mate's knee.

Canada's Gerald Ouellette was reported to have won the men's 50m rifle prone event in 1956 with a maximum score of 600. He kept the gold but the record was scrapped after the distance to the target was found to be 1.5m short.

Rey Robinson and Eddie Hart were tipped to challenge for medals in the men's 100m in 1972 and won their heats comfortably. But they missed the quarter-finals when the United States track coach misread the schedule, and they were out of the competition.

"It's the Olympics. You have to give it everything and go for gold."

British BMX competitor Shanaze Reade, after she went crashing out of the 2008 competition while trying to improve on her silver medal position

Athletes in the men's 3,000m steeplechase at Los Angeles in 1932 actually ran an additional lap of the track after the officials lost count of how many had been completed. Reports indicate the final placings did not change as a result of the error.

After his two rivals were disqualified Eric Moussambani of Equatorial Guinea had the pool to himself as he tried to set a qualifying time in a heat of the 100m freestyle at Sydney in 2000. He set a personal best but was more than a minute slower than the qualifying mark.

Hungarian heavyweight István Lévai was suspected by many observers of running away from Teófilo Stevenson when they met in the semi-final in Moscow in 1980. But the tactics worked as Lévai became the first Olympic boxer to go the distance with the Cuban powerhouse.

United States athletes were chasing a sprint relay double at the 2008 Games but saw their hopes wrecked when both the men's and women's teams dropped the baton and didn't even qualify for their respective finals.

Lori Jones was favourite to win the women's 100m hurdles in Beijing. But the American stumbled after clipping the 9th of 10 obstacles and trailed over the finish line in seventh place.

The American team failed to take into account the difference between the Greek and the Julian calendars when they planned their trip to the 1896 Games. Instead of arriving in Athens with 12 days in which to prepare, they arrived with the action due to begin the next day.

Nadia Comăneci beat the system when she came up with a perfect 10 in 1976. The gymnastics scoreboard in the Montreal Forum could only show three digits, so instead of 10.00 her score had to be displayed as 1.00.

A mix-up by officials led to the United States swimmers missing the semi-finals of the 100m freestyle in 1912. In a specially-arranged third heat Duke Kahanamoku beat the Olympic record he'd set earlier in the competition and then went on to win the final.

A judge's error deprived Canada's Sylvie Fréchette of gold in the 1992 synchronised swimming. The judge entered a score of 8.7 instead of 9.7 and Fréchette had to accept second place. After an appeal she was awarded a gold 16 months after the event.

Reports from the weightlifting events at Athens in 1896 tell of Games officials having trouble moving one of the weights during a break in competition. So Prince George of Greece, a member of the organising committee, bent down to help and easily lifted the weight.

Shirley Strickland was placed fourth in the 200m in 1948 but
judges failed to study the photo-finish results, which later
showed her in the bronze medal position. The Australian
declined to pursue the matter and went on to win seven
Olympic medals in total.

Wallace Spearmon of the United States and Churandy Martina
of the Dutch Antilles ran second and third respectively in
the men's 200m final in Beijing. However, Spearmon was
disqualified for stepping out of his lane and, having studied
the video, US officials insisted Martina be disqualified for the
same offence.

Ethiopian long-distance runner Miruts Yifter collected three
medals from Games appearances in 1972 and 1980 and might
have had another. He took bronze in the 10,000m in Munich
but arrived late for the 5,000m final and missed the race
completely.

Hammer thrower Declan Hegarty demolished the protective
cage when he lost control with his first attempt at Los Angeles
in 1984. Onlookers were confident of a better effort second
time round – but the Irishman did it again.

When Thomas Hamilton-Brown lost his opening lightweight
fight at the 1936 Games he consoled himself by embarking
on an eating binge. But when a scoring error emerged and
the South African was reinstated he was too heavy to
make the weight.

Race For The Line

1 *After Jean Boiteux of France won gold in the men's 400m freestyle swimming event in 1952, how is his father reported to have celebrated?*

2 *What was the nickname given to Eric Moussambani after his exploits in the men's 100m freestyle in Sydney?*

3 *How did Russian rower Vyacheslav Ivanov lose his gold medal after winning the single sculls at the 1956 Games?*

4 *Which team that set the second-fastest qualifying time in the women's 4x100m in Beijing also dropped the baton in the final?*

5 *The United States ended up with second and third places after two athletes were disqualified in the 2008 men's 200m, but what did Shawn Crawford do with his silver medal?*

6 *The Australian Olympic Committee blundered with the design of the medals for the 2000 Games in Sydney. Instead of the Parthenon in Athens, which ancient monument did they feature in the design?*

7 *Which team dropped the baton as they entered the last leg of the women's 4x100m with a commanding lead under the gaze of Adolf Hitler in 1936?*

8 *At which Games did Gail Devers win the 100m gold for the United States but slip to fifth when well placed to win after hitting the last obstacle in the 100m hurdles?*

9 *Dan O'Brien was tipped for decathlon gold in Atlanta by the United States athletes and his high-profile sponsors but he failed to make the team after a show of over-confidence saw him fail to set a score in which qualifying discipline?*

"I guess I dropped the stick. I thought my hand was there. Maybe someone has a voodoo doll of me."

American runner Lauryn Williams after she dropped the baton in the 4x100m in 2008

10 *Which diving legend athlete cracked his head on the springboard during the 1988 Games in Seoul, received stitches in the wound but continued to take the gold medal?*

11 *After testing positive for amphetamines, 65-year-old Paul Cerutti from Monaco was disqualified from the 1976 Games even though he finished 43rd out of 44 in which event?*

12 *Why did Richard Fanshawe of Great Britain and the Czech rider Otomar Bureš each incur thousands of penalty points during the eventing competition in 1936?*

Answers:

1   By jumping fully-clothed into the pool
2   Eric the Eel
3   He dropped it in the lake during his celebration
4   Jamaica
5   He gave it to Churandy Martina, who originally finished
    second
6   The Colosseum in Rome
7   Germany
8   Barcelona 1992
9   Pole vault
10 Greg Louganis
11 Trap shooting
12 They both had to chase their horses for several miles
    after falling

SHOCKS AND UPSETS

The ability of sport to deliver the unexpected is what makes it special – whatever the reason. A team or an individual can be tipped to take glory, then fail not because of a dropped baton or a foul but because the opponents raise their game or because things just don't work out.

There are times when injury or ill fortune open the door to the outsider, and others when the favourite runs out of steam. And there are occasions when the underdog has its day, although the natural tendency is to remember who lost on the big occasion rather than who struck to cause the upset that made the event so memorable.

Shock results at the Olympic Games have seen unfancied performers strike a blow for their emerging nation or for a sport in general against a dominant force. They have seen big-name athletes fail in their favoured competition, sometimes only to compensate by raising their game in their supposed weaker event. Occasionally the upsets extend across an Olympic career, when an athlete fails to claim the gold that their performances in another competition on another day would surely have delivered.

The emergence and then expansion of the Paralympics has given athletes with a disability the chance to demonstrate their courage and talent, and in recent years some have competed alongside able-bodied athletes with encouraging results. But they have some way to go to emulate the remarkable achievements of George Eyser.

41

20/12 Challenge

Warm-up Stretches

Reports suggest a train accident resulted in George Eyser
losing a leg. Whatever the cause, the German-born gymnast
overcame the handicap of a wooden leg to win three gold
medals, two silvers and a bronze for the United States at
the 1904 Games.

Japan were expected to make a clean sweep of the medals
when judo was introduced to the programme for the Games
in Tokyo in 1964, but they were denied by Dutchman Anton
Geesink who took gold in the open category.

Basketball was added to the Games schedule in 1936 and the
United States won gold every time – until their controversial
defeat by the Soviet Union in 1972 ended a run of seven gold
medals and 63 unbeaten matches.

Carl Schumann, a gymnast from Germany, stood only 5ft
4in tall but beat the big guys – starting with burly British
weightlifter Launceston Elliot – to win the wrestling
competition at the 1896 Games in Athens. Schumann also
took gold in three gymnastic events.

Gillian Sheen's foil success for Great Britain in 1956 even
surprised her country's media. Journalists didn't fancy her
chances of beating Olga Orban-Szabo, having lost to the
Romanian in an earlier bout, so they stayed away and
Sheen took the gold.

"I feel that by winning the silver it will make me crave the gold more and make me appreciate the gold more in the future so I think it is a good experience."

Park Sung-Hyun of South Korea, beaten favourite in women's individual archery in Beijing

From India's first victory in 1928 either they or Pakistan won a hockey medal at every Games – until 1988 when both nations missed out on the semi-finals.

Matt Biondi was denied a sixth gold medal in the pool at Seoul in 1988 by the unknown Anthony Nesty from Surinam. Nesty beat Biondi by a hundredth of a second in the 100m butterfly to take gold back to a country that had only one Olympic-size swimming pool.

Canada collected a gold medal at their first Olympics in Paris in 1900, but in Montreal in 1976 they became the first host nation to fail to win a single event.

British middle-distance runners Seb Coe and Steve Ovett won each other's best events in Moscow in 1980. Ovett upset the form book to triumph over 800m and was confident of success at his preferred distance of 1,500m six days later only for Coe to turn the tables.

Alberto Juantorena reportedly told his coach he only wanted
to run the 800m in Montreal as part of his training programme
for the 400m. In the event the Cuban took gold in both, setting
a world record at the longer distance.

Canada's Percy Williams had suffered from rheumatic fever
as a teenager and was advised to avoid strenuous exercise.
But that didn't stop him winning the sprint double in
Amsterdam in 1928 and equalling the Olympic record
for the 100m in the process.

The shock around 1,500m gold for Hicham El Guerrouj in
2004 was that it had taken so long. Having won four indoor
and outdoor world championship events, the Moroccan was
tipped for gold in Sydney but lost out to Noah Ngeny of Kenya.

Chinese fans were devastated when they turned up to witness
Liu Xiang begin his defence of the Olympic 110m hurdles title
in Beijing in 2008. After a false start by another athlete in the
first heat, the local hero pulled up with an Achilles injury and
was out of the Games.

Paula Radcliffe of Great Britain went into the women's
marathon in 2004 as the world record-holder and hot
favourite for gold. But the race proved too much for her and
she dropped out after 23 miles.

Cuba is second only to the United States in the all-time table
of Olympic boxing medals but they went home from Beijing
with only silver and bronze – the first time since 1968 that
they fought and failed to deliver gold.

The United States were on the end of a double basketball shock in 2004 when the men scraped into the knockout stages after defeats against Puerto Rico and Lithuania and were also beaten by eventual winners Argentina in the semi-final.

Nigeria became the first African nation to win the Olympic football tournament in 1996, beating Argentina in the final after a victory over Brazil in the semi-final.

Dave Wottle was unfancied in the final of the 800m in 1972 and duly slipped to the back of the field. But with just over a lap to go the American began making up ground on the favourite Yevgeniy Arzhanov to win by inches, with the Soviet star stumbling across the line in second.

After six Americans and one South African, Harold Abrahams of Great Britain became the first European to win the men's 100m when he edged Jackson Scholz of the United States in Paris in 1924.

Abebe Bikila of Ethiopia was the shock winner of the marathon in Rome in 1960 – not least because he completed the course barefoot. He wore shoes when he won a record second consecutive Olympic marathon in 1964 and in a world-record time.

Race For The Line

1   *In which discontinued event did George Eyser win one of his gold medals in 1904?*

2   *The United States regained their basketball title in 1976 but who took advantage of the Moscow boycott to win it in 1980?*

3   *Which nation won hockey gold in Seoul in 1988 for the first time since 1920?*

4   *Which event did Paula Radcliffe also fail to finish five days after dropping out of the 2004 marathon?*

5   *Which Scottish runner and devout Christian pulled out of the 1924 men's 100m when he realised the final would be on a Sunday but instead went on to win bronze in the 200m and gold in the 400m?*

6   *Softball was only added to the Olympic schedule from Atlanta in 1996 – and predictably enough was dominated by the United States with three successive golds. But which country pulled off a shock result to win gold in 2008?*

7   *Which legendary Australian runner finished ninth in the 1964 marathon behind Abebe Bikila, was recognised for setting 17 world records at various distances, but had only one Olympic medal to show for his ability – bronze in the 10,000m in 1964?*

8   *How did the American Robert LeGendre come to set a world record for the long jump at the 1924 Games but only earn a bronze medal?*

"I've never before not been able to finish and I'm desperately trying to find a reason for what happened. I just feel numb – this is something I worked so hard for."

Paula Radcliffe after dropping out of the women's marathon in 2004

9   *Josy Barthel of Luxembourg was a surprise winner of the men's 1,500m in 1952 but which athlete who would later smash a running milestone record finished fourth?*

10   *After the United States basketball "Dream Team" of 1992 and "Nightmare Team" of 2004, what was the nickname of the squad that won gold in 2008?*

11   *Which African nation followed up Nigeria's soccer success with a penalty shoot-out win over Spain in 2000?*

12   *What was the item of clothing that became Dave Wottle's trademark during his running career?*

Answers:

1 Rope climbing
2 Yugoslavia
3 Great Britain
4 10,000m
5 Eric Liddell
6 Japan
7 Ron Clarke
8 His record jump came in the pentathlon
9 Roger Bannister
10 The Redeem Team
11 Cameroon
12 A golf cap

HEROES AND VILLAINS

There will always be more notice paid to the villains than the heroes, partly because the bad guys always hit the headlines hardest but also because when someone does the right thing in the Olympic Games people are generally entitled to expect no less.

Participation in the Games is taken as acceptance that a performer will make the necessary sacrifices rather than expect special treatment even if they are committed, talented and fortunate enough to win gold.

So the richest praise goes to the competitors who scale the heights not necessarily by dominating their events but by performing – win or lose – with good grace and with respect for their opponents, the officials and the spectators. It extends also to those notables for whom success at the Games was only part of a remarkable life story of true life and death heroism.

Sometimes those branded as villains can claim with some justification to have been let down by others, misrepresented or just victims of unfortunate error or heat-of-the-moment reactions. Others have been exposed as cheats, plain and simple, regardless of the level of mechanical or pharmaceutical sophistication behind their dishonesty.

But the real heartbreak comes from the feeling of total emptiness endured by true sports fans on seeing an athlete at the peak of their powers deliver a performance worthy of the gold medal, the world record and the adulation of millions. Only to then find it was chemically assisted.

20/12 Challenge

Warm-up Stretches

"German sport has only one task: to strengthen the character of the German people, imbuing it with the fighting spirit and steadfast camaraderie necessary in the struggle for its existence."

Joseph Goebbels, Hitler's Minister of Propaganda, on his sporting priorities

American weightlifter Harold Sakata was a hero with a silver medal in the 1948 Games but a villain in the very best traditions as the baddie "Oddjob" in the 1964 James Bond film Goldfinger.

Ben Johnson destroyed the field and produced one of the most spectacular performances in Olympic history to win the 100m in Seoul in a world-record time of 9.79 seconds, but his betrayal was exposed three days later when he was revealed to have failed a drugs test.

French cyclist Robert Charpentier beat team-mate Guy Lapébie by 0.2 seconds at the end of the 100km race in 1936. Lapébie suddenly slowed down but a photograph later showed his shirt had been tugged by his opponent.

Léon Flameng emerged as a true sporting hero when his
opponent's bike broke down in a cycling event in 1896.
Flameng dismounted, waited for the Greek's replacement
bike to arrive and then resumed. He still won by six laps.

Jesse Owens was undoubtedly the hero of the 1936 Games in
Berlin, not least because his success was achieved under the
gaze of German Chancellor Adolf Hitler, one of the biggest
villains of all time.

Korean boxer Jung-Il Byun refused to leave the ring after losing
a decision in the bantamweight division at the 1988 Games. He
remained alone in the ring for more than an hour, long after
officials had turned off the lights and left the building.

American runner Marion Jones was the first woman to win
five medals at a single Games in Sydney with a sprint double
plus gold in the 4x400 relay and bronze in the 4x100 and
the long jump. But she was stripped of all the medals after
admitting taking steroids.

The East German authorities emerged as the villains behind
a state-sponsored drugs programme. Following reunification
with West Germany it emerged that doping of East German
athletes had been carried out on athletes of all ages and in
all sports, with silence guaranteed by the involvement of the
secret police, the Stasi.

Swedish wrestler Ara Abrahamian threw his bronze medal to
the floor in protest at the referee after he lost his 84kg Greco-
Roman semi-final in 2008. The IOC responded by stripping
him of the medal.

Boris Onishchenko was disqualified from the modern pentathlon fencing stage in 1976 after it was discovered he had tampered with his epee, enabling him to register a score without actually hitting anything. The Soviet team was forced to withdraw as a result.

Cuba's Ángel Valodia Matos, a taekwondo gold medallist in Sydney, was banned for life by the sport's federation after he was disqualified in 2008 for exceeding the injury time-limit – and responded by kicking the referee in the head.

George Smith Patton became one of America's greatest military heroes and also made his mark on the Olympics. He finished fifth in the modern pentathlon at the 1912 Games. It was later noted that shooting was the future general's weakest event.

Avery Brundage was revered by many as head of the US Olympic Committee and later as President of the IOC, but he was also criticised for his reluctance to allow women to compete in the Games and was branded a racist for his treatment of black and Jewish athletes.

Philip Neame was the classic boy's own hero. He earned the Victoria Cross in the First World War, won a shooting gold for Great Britain at the 1924 Olympics, survived being mauled by a tiger, escaped from a German prison in the Second World War and was later knighted.

Hungary's Károly Takács, a world-class marksman, responded in heroic style when a faulty grenade blew off his right hand in 1938. He switched to his left hand and won gold in the 25m rapid-fire pistol in 1948 and again in 1952.

Fans and team-mates turned on Australian rower Sally Robbins when she dropped her oar and slumped back onto a colleague in the final of the women's eight in 2004. Other crew members branded her a quitter but were criticised themselves by officials for their hostile reaction.

Zola Budd was booed by fans in Los Angeles after she clashed with American star Mary Decker in the 3,000m steeplechase. Decker went tumbling off the track after running into the back of the adopted Briton. Budd finished seventh, was disqualified but then reinstated after officials viewed a recording of the race.

American fury was directed at match officials when their team lost the basketball final to the Soviet Union in 1972. The game ended in chaos with disputes over added time and time-outs but the Soviets kept their cool to score the decisive basket and win 51–50.

Three judges were suspended after rising star of the boxing ring Roy Jones Jr lost the 1988 light-middleweight final to Park Si-Hun. The bout was so one-sided that the Korean apologised to Jones and a judge later admitted there had been an error, but the result stood.

Black Ethiopian runner Derartu Tulu ran her victory lap hand in hand with second-placed white South African Elana Meyer when the pair completed the 10,000m in 1992. The show of unity marked the end of South Africa's isolation from the Games and brought the crowd to their feet.

Race For The Line

1 *What substance did Hans-Gunnar Liljenwall admit to taking to calm his nerves prior to a shooting round in the 1968 modern pentathlon – leading to Sweden losing the team bronze for drug use?*

2 *What was unusual about Zola Budd's running style?*

3 *What was the nickname bestowed on Sally Robbins by her angry team-mates?*

4 *What is the name of the trophy awarded to the best boxing stylist of a Games, and presented to Roy Jones Jr after the shock decision by the judges in 1988?*

5 *What was the nationality of Bakhaava Buidaa, who won judo silver in 1972 but was stripped of the medal after failing a drugs test?*

6 *Finland's Martti Vainio won long-distance running medals in the 1983 World Championships and the European Championships of 1978 and 1982, but in which Olympics was he disqualified after a positive drugs test?*

7 *Zbigniew Kaczmarek of Poland and Blagoi Blagoev of Bulgaria in 1976 were among the first Olympic medallists in which sport to be disqualified for drug use?*

8 *Ukrainian athlete Lyudmila Blonska was stripped of her silver medal at the 2008 Games after testing positive for steroids. She was also banned from competing in the final of which additional event?*

"I have been dishonest, and you have the right to be angry with me. I have let my family down, I have let my country down and I have let myself down."

Marion Jones, owning up to her drug use

9 *After allegations of professionalism led to record-breaking American athlete Jim Thorpe being controversially stripped of his double gold from the 1912 Games, which IOC official who had been beaten by Thorpe in Stockholm led opposition to calls for the medals to be reinstated?*

10 *Why was Chinese gymnast Dong Fangxiao stripped of her bronze medal from the Sydney Games in 2000?*

11 *How did Greek athletes Kostas Kenteris and Katerina Thanou attempt to cover their tracks after missing a drugs test during the Athens Olympics in 2004?*

12 *Which American athlete was upgraded from gold to silver after Ben Johnson's disqualification in 1988?*

Answers:

1   Two beers
2   She normally ran barefoot
3   Lay Down Sally
4   The Val Barker Trophy
5   Mongolian
6   Los Angeles in 1984
7   Weightlifting
8   Long jump
9   Avery Brundage
10 She was found to be too young to compete
11 They faked a motorcycle accident
12 Carl Lewis

IN THE FAMILY

Family partnerships are less common in modern top-level sport, but sibling success has been quite prevalent over more than 100 years of the Olympics.

With the notable exceptions of the Williams sisters Venus and Serena, and fellow American tennis doubles stars Bob and Mike Bryan, most of the family partnerships have come in the lesser-known sports, although British brothers Reginald and Lawrence Doherty won the men's doubles tennis competition in 1900.

In some cases a family has made its mark in a particular event, often over two or three generations, such as the Gerevich family fencers and the Lunde sailors from Norway. In others, couples have claimed Olympic glory as man and wife, or have married after meeting as a result of their sporting careers.

There are many stories of sibling success and some remarkable tales of twins taking gold – on one occasion against another set. Families have lined up in team games and in small crews, and even members of royal families have played a part.

On occasions siblings have squared up against each other in a head-to-head with gold at stake, but contests pitching parent against child are rare. Only Margaret Abbott will know if it is ever a good idea to beat your mother at golf, whether you know it's an Olympic final or not.

20/12 Challenge

Warm-up Stretches

"It always has to be a team to co-operate, and to be friends. We will keep competing for as long as we can."

Peter Hochschorner who, with brother Pavol, has won three Olympic canoeing golds for Slovakia

Margaret Abbott became the first American woman to win an Olympic event with first place in women's golf in 1900. Her mother Mary finished seventh. But organisation of the event was so haphazard that it was only identified as an Olympic tournament following research after Margaret's death.

Marion and Georgina Jones of the United States became the first sisters to compete in the Games in the tennis tournament of 1900. Marion came third in the singles and fourth in the mixed doubles but Georgina lost in the first round of both. There was no women's doubles competition.

Soviet sisters Irina and Tamara Press were athletics stars of the early 1960s. Irina won 80m hurdles gold in Rome and pentathlon gold in Tokyo. Tamara won the shot put at both Games plus discus gold in Tokyo and silver in the same event in Rome. But suspicion shrouded their achievements, especially when they stopped competing after the introduction of gender tests.

Michelle Capes and her sister Lee were members of
the Australian hockey team that won gold in 1988. The
Netherlands also boasted siblings in their bronze-medal
teams: Carina Benninga lined up in the Dutch women's team
and younger brother Marc played for the men.

Aladár Gerevich was a Hungarian fencing legend in his own
right. In addition to his success, wife Erna Bogen won foil
bronze in 1932, father-in-law Albert won team sabre silver in
1912 and son Pal won team sabre bronze in 1972 and 1980.

Italian brothers Nedo and Aldo Nadi won nine fencing
medals between them in the same Games. Nedo, older by five
years, won gold in the individual foil and sabre events and
in all three team competitions in 1920. Aldo won gold in the
three team events and silver – beaten by his brother – in the
individual sabre.

John and Sumner Paine of the United States were the first
brothers to both win gold in the Games. Sumner came first
in the free pistol competition in 1896 and was beaten into
second place by John in the military revolver event.

The French crew of the vessel Mac Miche, which won gold
in the 6m sailing class at the 1912 Games in Stockholm,
comprised the Thubé brothers, Gaston, Jacques and Amédée.

Swedish marksman Oscar Swahn won three golds, a silver and
two bronze medals in a shooting career spanning the 1908,
1912 and 1920 Games. He was accompanied throughout by
son Alfred, who won three gold, two silver and a bronze and
who added a silver and two bronze in 1924.

The first known twins to win gold medals were the Carlberg brothers from Sweden at the 1912 Games in Stockholm. Vilhelm won the 25m small-bore rifle event and was joined by Eric for team success in the same category and the 30m military pistol competiton.

East German twins Jörg and Bernd Landvoigt won the coxless pair gold medal at the 1980 Games and beat Soviet twins Yuri and Nikolay Pimenov into second place.

Walter Jakobsson of Finland and his German-born wife Ludowika were the first married couple to win gold in a winter sport – and they did it at a summer Games. The pair took first place in figure skating when it formed part of the schedule at Antwerp in 1920.

Soviet twins Anatoli and Sergei Beloglazov shared success in Olympic wrestling. Anatoli won gold in 1980 in the 52k division. Sergei won in 1980 and again in 1988 in the bantamweight class.

Members of the Roycroft family were ever-present in the Australian Olympic team from 1960 until 1988. Bill won gold in the eventing team in 1960 and, with son Wayne, took bronze in 1968 and 1976. Other sons Clarke and Barry also competed, as did Wayne's wife Vicki.

The Keller family was prominent in Germany's hockey success over a period of nearly 60 years. Erwin was in the team that won silver in Berlin in 1936, son Carsten was in the gold-winning team in 1972 and grandson Andreas contributed to another gold in 1992.

Dezső Gyarmati won three golds, a silver and a bronze with the Hungarian water polo team between 1948 and 1964. Wife Éva Székely won a gold and a silver for breaststroke in 1952 and 1956 respectively and their daughter Andrea won silver and bronze in backstroke and butterfly in 1972.

Max and Marie Decugis were the first married couple to win gold when they partnered in the tennis mixed doubles for France in 1906, but these were the Intercalated Games and the medals are not recognised by the IOC.

Peder Lunde of Norway became the third generation of his family to pick up a sailing medal when his team won the Flying Dutchman class in 1960. Parents Peder and Vibeke had won silver in the 5.5m class in 1952 and grandfather Eugen had won gold in the 6m class in 1924.

Two sets of twins delivered wrestling gold for the United States as they hosted the 1984 Games in Los Angeles. Dave and Mark Schultz were the first to achieve the feat with gold in the 74kg event and the 82kg class respectively. Ed Banach won at 90kg and his twin Lou won the 100kg category.

Spain's future king Juan Carlos competed in yachting in 1972. Daughter Cristina took part in the 1988 tornado class and son Felipe was in the Soling class at the Barcelona Games. Their uncle, King Constantine of Greece, had won a sailing gold in 1960, when their mother also competed.

Race For The Line

1 *For what reason did Zara Phillips pull out of the 2004 and 2008 Olympics, missing the chance to emulate her mother, Princess Anne, who competed in 1976, and her father, Mark Phillips, who won eventing gold in 1972?*

2 *John Kelly of the United States won single sculls gold in 1920 and partnered his cousin to victory in the double sculls, but who was his film star daughter?*

3 *Sandra Henderson and Stephane Préfontaine played an important part at the 1976 Games in Montreal and were later married. What was their role at the Games?*

4 *What was the surname of American athletes Al, who won triple jump gold in 1984, and sister Jackie, who became a serial Olympic medal winner from 1984 to 1996?*

5 *For which nation did husband and wife Garry and Kathy Cook win track medals at the 1984 Games?*

6 *Which post did Wayne Roycroft hold with Australia's Olympic eventing team from 1988 until 2010?*

7 *In which event did brothers Dhyan Chand Singh and Roop Singh win five golds between them for India between 1928 and 1936?*

8 *Gina Hemphill ran the final leg of the torch relay in 1984. Which legendary athlete was her grandfather?*

9 *In which category did Germany's representatives Max and Bruno Götze become the first brothers to win a cycling medal, with silver in 1906?*

"I can't imagine having a pro career without Serena. She inspires me. She taught me how to dig deep, be a fighter."

Venus Williams, who partnered her sister to Olympic tennis doubles gold

10 *For which nation did Miklós Németh win gold in the javelin in 1976, emulating the success of his father Imre, who won hammer gold in 1948 and bronze in 1952?*

11 *What was the nickname bestowed on Irina and Tamara Press by members of the media who doubted their gender?*

12 *At the Sydney Games in 2000 Hazel and Joetta Clark and their sister-in-law Jearl Miles-Clark all represented the United States in the semi-final of which track event?*

Answers:

1 Injury to her horse, Toytown
2 Grace Kelly
3 Carrying the Olympic torch
4 Joyner
5 Great Britain
6 Head coach
7 Hockey
8 Jesse Owens
9 Tandem
10 Hungary
11 The Press Brothers
12 800m

TRACK STARS

For many people the men's 100m is the highlight of the Olympics – a four-year wait followed by the briefest and most concentrated burst of power. How many worthwhile things can a person do in 9.69 seconds?

The progression of the world record – or lack of it – from Jim Hines's altitude-assisted 9.95 seconds in 1968 to Usain Bolt's time 40 years on gives an idea of the fine margins between success and failure, as does the fact that only four of the finalists in 2008 were faster than Hines.

In the longer and slower events pace still plays a part but stamina comes into play more. The Finns of the 1950s dominated distance running, and more recently those events have provided the platform for African nations to build great sporting traditions.

Technique is always important. There is no shortage of top sprinters who have hit hurdles or dropped batons, and in walking the offence of "lifting" – the failure to maintain contact with the track – brings disqualifications even at the highest level.

And increasingly a strong nerve is vital. One can only wonder how the 1912 men's 100m final would have ended up if a zero-tolerance policy had been in place for false starts.

20/12 Challenge

Warm-up Stretches

"It was the only time in my life that I finished a race and felt absolutely dead."

Jim Hines, after winning the 100m in Mexico in 1968 with a world-record time of 9.95 seconds

Usain Bolt exploded out of the starting blocks to win gold in the 100m in a new world-record time of 9.69 seconds. Four days later he did it again, winning the 200m in a record time of 19.30 seconds. A third world record of 37.10 came when Bolt led Jamaica to gold in the 4x100m.

Ralph Craig admitted to one false start in the 100m in 1912 and was blamed by some sources for three of the seven infringements that delayed the race. But there were no penalties at the time and the American sprinted to take the gold, adding the 200m title four days later.

The women's walking event was increased from 10km to 20km in 2000 and the gold went to China's Wang Liping – but only after three leading competitors were disqualified for lifting. First to go was Liu Hongyu of China, then the 1996 silver medallist at 10km Elisabetta Perrone of Italy. Jane Saville of Australia was inside the stadium when she was stopped.

Men have contested a 20km walk since 1965 and a 50km event since 1932. Robert Korzeniowski of Poland won at 20km in 2000, the same year that he won his second of three consecutive golds for the 50km race.

No woman has won the marathon twice since it was introduced in 1984, but Valentina Yegorova came close. She took gold for the Unified Team in 1992 and four years later finished second, two minutes behind Fatuma Roba of Ethiopia.

After winning marathon gold in 1972, Frank Shorter of the United States set off again four years later to try and emulate Abebe Bikila, the first man to win twice. But Shorter came second to Waldemar Cierpinski, and it was the East German who then went on to secure a second win in 1980.

Stricken by polio as a child, Wilma Rudolph couldn't walk properly until she was 11. But at the age of 16 she won a bronze medal with the United States sprint relay team in Melbourne and in 1960 she swept the board in Rome, winning the sprint double and the relay.

Lina Radke of Germany won the first 800m event for women in 1928 but the distance was then dropped from the schedule because of concerns that it was too challenging. It returned in 1960, by which time the Soviets were dominant and Lyudmila Lisenko won gold.

Fanny Blankers-Koen capped a record-breaking performance at the 1948 Games by leading the Dutch team to gold in the 4x100m. She had already won individual gold in the 100m and 200m as well as in the 80m hurdles.

Cathy Freeman was chosen to light the Olympic flame when
the Games arrived in Sydney. She also carried the hopes
of the Australian people – particularly those of Aboriginal
descent – in the 400m. She didn't disappoint, winning the
gold medal to go with her silver from 1996.

Hannes Kolehmainen was the first of Finland's famed distance
runners, winning the 5,000m and 10,000m double in 1912 as
well as the cross-country. He added the marathon in 1920.

Paavo Nurmi picked up where Kolehmainen left off, winning
three gold medals in 1920 and adding six more in 1924 and
1928 at distances from 1,500m to 10,000m and cross-country.
Ville Ritola won five long-distance medals at the same Games.
Years later Lasse Virén revived the tradition, winning the
5,000m and 10,000m double in Munich and Montreal.

Harrison Dillard was the favourite for the high hurdles in 1948
but missed out on selection for the United States team after
falling during the trials. He switched to the 100m and led from
start to finish in London to take gold.

Tirunesh Dibaba of Ethiopia became the first woman to win
the double of 5,000m and 10,000m. The cousin of Derartu
Tulu, who won the 10,000m in 1992 and 2000, and sister of
Ejegayehu, who took 10,000m silver in 2004, Tirunesh won
5,000m bronze in 2004 and took the double in 2008.

In 1948 the legendary Czech runner Emil Zátopek lapped all
but the silver and bronze medallists in winning the 10,000m.
Four years later he won the event again and also added gold
in the 5,000m and the marathon.

British runner Chris Brasher was disqualified for brushing past Norway's Ernst Larsen on his way to first place in the 3,000m steeplechase in 1956. But the medal was reinstated after other runners including Larsen supported Brasher in his appeal.

The men's 4x400m in 2000 took less than three minutes to run but eight years to decide. The United States finished first but were disqualified in 2004 because of drug use by Jerome Young. In 2005 they were reinstated – and in 2008 disqualified again when another team member, Antonio Pettigrew, admitted drugs offences.

The last time the United States lost the 4x400m in a straight race was 1952. Prior to the 2000 doping scandal, the Americans stayed away from Moscow in 1980 and couldn't field a team in Munich in 1972 after two runners were suspended for showing disrespect during an earlier medal ceremony.

Irena Szewińska specialised in world records, setting one for each of her gold medals. She started with gold in the Polish team in the 4x100m in Tokyo, added the 200m gold in Mexico and took the 400m gold in Montreal. She also won two silvers in 1964 and bronze in 1968 and 1972.

Belgian officials were caught out in 1920 when the 110m hurdles in Antwerp was won by the Canadian runner Tommy Thomson. They couldn't find the Canadian flag so flew the Union Jack instead.

Race For The Line

1 *Which Russian athlete in 1972 became the first European to win the men's sprint double?*

2 *For which nation did Brimin Kipruto win a seventh successive men's 3,000m steeplechase in 2008?*

3 *Which European nation took silver in the 100m in 2004, thereby preventing a clean sweep of medals at 100m, 200m and 400m by the United States men?*

4 *In which event did Tirunesh Dibaba's husband, Sileshi Sihine, win silver for Ethiopia in 2004 and 2008?*

5 *Which Scottish runner in 1980 became the first British athlete to win the men's 100m since Harold Abrahams in 1924?*

6 *For which South American nation did Jefferson Pérez win a first Olympic medal by taking gold in the 20km walk in 1996?*

7 *Who in 2004 became the first woman to win the 800m and the 1,500m at the same Games?*

8 *Hassiba Boulmerka won gold at 1,500m in 1992, but why was she singled out for criticism by some in her home country of Algeria?*

9 *For which nation did Renate Stecher win a total of six sprint medals, including three golds and a sprint double, at the Games in 1972 and 1976?*

10 *How did the media refer to Finland's highly successful long-distance runners?*

> *"I came here to prove that I'm the best in the world and I did it."*

Usain Bolt, after winning the 100m in Beijing in 2008 with a world-record time of 9.69 seconds

11 *What was the nickname bestowed on Fanny Blankers-Koen?*

12 *Which legendary United States sprinter capped his career with long jump gold in Atlanta but was not selected for the 4x100m, which the Americans subsequently lost to Canada?*

Answers:

1 Valeri Borzov
2 Kenya
3 Portugal
4 10,000m
5 Allan Wells
6 Ecuador
7 Kelly Holmes
8 For running with her legs uncovered
9 East Germany
10 The Flying Finns
11 The Flying Housewife
12 Carl Lewis

FIELD OF DREAMS

Evidence of the increasingly tough competition in field events is provided by the shortage of multiple medallists. The days of Ray Ewry and Martin Sheridan – and even of Al Oerter and Viktor Saneyev – are long gone, and competitors in the modern age are lucky to win two golds in their discipline, never mind three or four.

Unlike the runners, few jumping and throwing specialists are given a second chance by way of a different version of their own event, or a team competition. Some have shown a talent for long jump and triple jump – and on occasions high jump as well. Others have demonstrated that they can throw anything a long way given the chance, but the modern trend has been to focus on one event to the exclusion of all else.

Domination by particular nations, which was certainly evident in the women's events, has also eased if only because the break-up of the Soviet Union has brought the emergence of new countries. Ukraine, Belarus, Estonia, Lithuania and Latvia all won medals in field events in Beijing. The United States – never a force in women's field events – has seen a decline in its success in the men's equivalents since the 1960s and certainly since the early 1900s, when on occasions the Americans only had to turn up to win.

Serious competition from talented athletes representing more nations is definitely good for the Games, even if some of the winners do sometimes have to wait a few months for their medals.

20/12 Challenge

Warm-up Stretches

From 1900 until 1912 the Games featured standing versions
of the three jumping events. Ray Ewry of the United States
won all three in Paris and St Louis. When the triple jump
was dropped after 1904, he won the other two events at the
Intercalated Games and again in 1908. His record of 10 golds
stood until 2008.

Al Oerter was the first man to throw a discus further than
200 feet and always raised his game at the Olympics. He
won gold at Melbourne in 1956 and went on to become the
first track and field athlete to win the same event at four
consecutive Games.

The United States won the men's pole vault twice between
1972 and 2008 – but prior to that they only failed to win gold
once in 17 attempts. Fernand Gonder of France interrupted
their run by taking gold at the Intercalated Games in 1906.

The women's pole vault was added to the schedule in 2000.
Yelena Isinbayeva finished well down the field but would
return to dominate the event. The Russian took gold in 2004
and 2008, sealing victory in Beijing with a world-record
height of 5.05m.

Jan Železný lost out to Finland's Tapio Korjus by 16
centimetres in the battle for javelin gold in 1988. But the
Czech returned to win the event at the next three Games.

"Compared to this jump, we are all children."

Soviet long jumper Igor Ter-Ovanesyan, reflecting on Bob Beamon's record-breaking leap at Mexico in 1968

Tatyana Lebedeva of Russia won long jump gold in 2004 and followed it with silver in 2008. She also won three triple jump medals but gold evaded her. In 2000 she was beaten by Teresa Marinova of Bulgaria and in 2004 Françoise Mbango Etone won a first athletics gold for Cameroon, repeating the success in 2008.

John Flanagan of the United States won the first three men's hammer competitions between 1900 and 1908. Ireland's Pat O'Callaghan in 1928 and 1932 and Soviet athlete Yuriy Sedykh in 1976 and 1980 are the only other men to have won more than once.

The only man to win the high jump and the long jump was Ellery Clark, who took both titles for the United States at the first Games in 1896. A Harvard graduate, Clark won the long jump final with his last chance after two foul jumps.

Irish-born Martin Sheridan competed for the United States and won nine Olympic medals including five golds. Five of his medals came at the Intercalated Games: gold for shot and discus, silver for stone throw and standing high and long jumps.

Soviet triple jumper Viktor Saneyev missed out by
11 centimetres on winning a fourth gold medal. Saneyev won
gold at his first Games in 1968 and repeated the achievement
in 1972 and 1976 but was beaten by compatriot Jaak Uudmäe
in Moscow.

Nina Romashkova became the first Soviet athlete to win
Olympic gold with first place in the discus in 1952. She had to
settle for bronze in 1956 but regained her title in 1960.

After missing out on long jump gold in 1900, Meyer Prinstein
won the event in 1904 and 1906. The American also won triple
jump gold in 1900 and 1904.

Ulrike Meyfarth of West Germany became the youngest
winner of an athletics event when she took gold in the high
jump in 1972 at the age of 16. She failed to reach the final in
Montreal and didn't go to Moscow but won gold again in the
same event in 1984.

Koji Murofushi of Japan was the double beneficiary of drugs
cheats. The Japanese hammer-thrower took gold in 2004 after
the disqualification of Hungary's Adrián Annus. When two
were disqualified four years later he was elevated to
bronze – but not until four months after the event.

Bob Beamon leapt into long jump history with his first
attempt in the thin air of Mexico in 1968. Beamon recorded 29
feet two and a half inches. His second jump was nowhere near
as impressive but it didn't matter because the gold medal –
and the world record – were Beamon's.

Ellina Zvereva of Belarus was at her third Games when in 2000 she became the oldest women to claim athletics gold, winning the discus at 39 years and 316 days. She continued to compete and in 2008 finished sixth at the age of 47.

A boycott and then injury denied legendary pole vaulter Sergey Bubka the chance to compete at the 1984 and 1996 Games. In the three editions that he did attend, Bubka won one medal – gold in 1988 as the Soviet Union completed a clean sweep in the event.

Mary Rand's long jump success in 1964 was Great Britain's first gold in women's athletics. On the same day, Welshman Lynn Davies made it a British double by taking gold in the men's event.

Ruth Fuchs in 1976 became the only woman to win two gold medals in the women's javelin, having also won in 1972. The East German was considered the best in her event during the 1970s but she later admitted to having been part of the state-sponsored drug programme.

Tamara Press is the only double winner in the women's shot put, taking gold in 1960 and 1964. Fellow Soviets Galina Zybina in 1956 and Nadezhda Chizhova in 1976 both followed gold with silver, as did East Germany's Margitta Gummel in 1972.

Race For The Line

1 Which athlete who never managed better than silver in the Olympics finally beat Bob Beamon's long jump world record in the 1991 World Championships?

2 Which former Soviet nation dominated the men's discus from 1992, with two golds and a bronze for Virgilijus Alekna and a gold for Romas Ubartas?

3 In which event introduced for women in 2000 did Russia's Olga Kuzenkova win the first silver medal before adding gold in 2004?

4 Ray Ewry's jumping success was the result of him strengthening his legs after contracting which illness as a child?

5 Which field event did Dana Zátopková win in 1952 on the same day that husband Emil won the 5,000m?

6 Which athlete won Olympic gold in the high jump in 1968 with a technique which revolutionised the event?

7 Which is the only nation other than the United States to win back-to-back gold medals in the men's pole vault, with success in 1976 and 1980?

8 In 1984 Great Britain took two women's javelin medals with Tessa Sanderson winning gold and Fatima Whitbread taking bronze. What was the nationality of Tiina Lillak, who won silver?

9 For which nation did Yumileidi Cumbá in 2004 become the first non-European woman to win gold in the shot put?

"I don't compete with other discus throwers. I compete with my own history."

Al Oerter, who recorded a career-best in three of his four Olympic discus victories

10 *Which athlete in 2000 became the first from Great Britain to win triple jump gold since Tim Ahearne in 1908?*

11 *In which field event did Lia Manoliu twice win bronze for Romania before finally taking gold in 1968 in the fifth of her six appearances at the Games?*

12 *For which European nation did Tia Hellebaut – jumping while wearing spectacles – win a first women's high jump gold in 2008?*

Answers:

1 Mike Powell
2 Lithuania
3 Hammer
4 Polio
5 Javelin
6 Dick Fosbury with the Fosbury Flop
7 Poland
8 Finnish
9 Cuba
10 Jonathan Edwards
11 Discus
12 Belgium

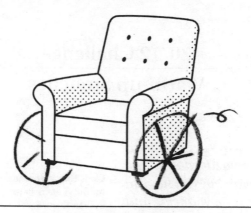

TWO WHEELS

One of only a handful of ever-present events at the Olympics, cycling has changed enormously over the years since France dominated the 1896 competition. The French still lead the medal table and won't be overhauled any time soon – not least because, in addition to the more traditional events, they have shown their ability in the more modern disciplines of mountain biking and BMX.

Italy have been a force on two wheels since winning their first gold in 1920, and Great Britain confirmed their resurgence in the sport with 14 medals in Beijing – the highest total since the 21 won by the United States in an uncompetitive event in 1904 skewed their position in the medal table.

Cycling has seen riders dicing with danger and with drugs, sometimes at the same time. Maurice Peeters became the oldest gold medallist in 1920 and was on course to set a new record four years later until apparently suffering from the effects of having begun his celebrations before the event started.

More recently Jeannie Longo set records in the 2008 Games for age and longevity in women's cycling. She contested the road race just a few months short of her 50th birthday – 24 years older than the gold medallist, Great Britain's Nicole Cooke.

20/12 Challenge

Warm-up Stretches

"It's been such an amazing day for the team but you have to focus on your ride and think about the stuff that's happening to you."

Chris Hoy after a successful day for the Great Britain cyclists in 2008

France dominated the cycling events at the first Games in 1896 with Paul Masson winning the sprint, the time trial and the 10k. His countryman Léon Flameng was second in the 10km and third in the sprint but took first place in the 100km.

Only one cycle race took place at the 1912 Games in Stockholm but it turned out to be the longest in Olympic history. Rudolph Lewis of South Africa was first home – more than 10 hours after starting the 320km course.

Miguel Indurain of Spain was the first five-time winner of the Tour de France to win gold at the Olympics. He won gold in the 52km men's individual time trial in 1996, the year after his fifth Tour success.

British cyclist Chris Boardman caught reigning world champion Jens Lehmann of Germany with a full lap to go in winning the 4km pursuit final in 1992.

Chris Hoy's achievement in winning three cycling gold medals for Great Britain in 2008 equalled a record dating back 100 years, when Henry Taylor claimed three swimming medals for Great Britain in London.

Mountain bike racing was introduced to the Games schedule in 1996. Bart Brentjens of the Netherlands won the men's event and Paola Pezzo of Italy took gold in the women's competition.

After more than 220km, only 0.02 second separated the first three from an initial entry of 183 in the 1996 men's road race – the biggest field in any Olympic competition. Pascal Richard of Switzerland took gold, followed by the Dane Rolf Sørensen and Max Sciandri of Great Britain.

Bradley Wiggins of Great Britain equalled Burton Downing's record of six men's cycling medals when he added two in Beijing. With three golds, Wiggins has one more than the American, whose achievement came in the controversial 1904 Games when the United States faced no overseas competition of note.

Rebecca Romero became the first British woman to win medals in two different sports when she took cycling pursuit gold in 2008 to add to her rowing silver from 2004.

In 1972 Spain's Jaime Huélamo and Aad van den Hoek of the Netherlands became the first cyclists to be stripped of their medals after failing drugs tests. Huélamo had come third in the road race and van den Hoek third in the 100km team event.

Davide Rebellin of Italy was stripped of his silver from the 2008 men's road race more than a year after the event when re-tests of samples found a banned substance. The German cyclist Stefan Schumacher was also disqualified after the re-tests but had not finished in a medal place.

Dutch tandem pair Gerard Bosch van Drakestein and Maurice Peeters were well placed in the 1924 final but suddenly lost control and finished third behind France and Denmark. Van Drakestein later explained that Peeters often drank a glass of cognac before each race but had emptied the entire bottle before the final!

Ian Browne and Anthony Marchant of Australia had never ridden together until a few weeks before the 1956 Games and made a poor start on the tandem. They lost the first heat and then the repêchage but seized the last chance offered by a re-run, where they embarked on a winning streak all the way to the gold medal.

The United States captured three of the six medals when BMX racing made its Games debut in 2008. But they couldn't catch Māris Štrombergs of Latvia, who took gold in the men's event, or the French pair of Anne-Caroline Chausson and Laëtitia Le Corguillé, first and second respectively in the women's race.

Swedish brothers Gösta, Erik and Sture Pettersson were joined by Sven Hamrin to take bronze in the 1964 team time trial. Four years later Hamrin made way for the fourth brother, Tomas, and the Petterssons cycled to the silver medal.

Leontien van Moorsel overcame the effects of anorexia and bulimia to become the most successful woman cyclist at a single Games. The Dutch rider won three golds in Sydney plus a silver. In Athens she fell while defending her road race title but won a second gold in the time trial and added a bronze in the pursuit.

Soviet cyclist Viktor Kapitonov lost count of the laps in the 1960 road race and sprinted for the line too early. But Kapitonov had just enough left to hold off the challenge of Livio Trapè and deny Italy a clean sweep of all six cycling gold medals.

Robert Charpentier reportedly began his amateur cycling career as an apprentice butcher, using pedal power to make his deliveries. He ended it in 1936 by winning three gold medals at the Olympics: an individual in the men's road race plus two team firsts for France in the road race and the 4,000m pursuit.

Félicia Ballanger's gold in the time trial at Sydney made her the first woman to win three cycling gold medals only days before Leontien van Moorsel set her record of three golds in one Games. Ballanger also won the sprint in Sydney to go with her gold from the same event in Atlanta.

Jeannie Longo of France competed in a record seventh Games in 2008 and would have entered more had cycling been open to women pre-1984. She was the oldest women's cycling gold medallist when she won the road race in 1996 at 37 and 264 days.

Race For The Line

1 Which two-wheeled event was a demonstration sport at the 1908 Games in London?

2 Which engineering company more commonly associated with making sports cars manufactured the high-tech cycle used by Chris Boardman at the 1992 Games?

3 What happened in 1996 to change the face of the Olympic cycling competition?

4 Which legendary cyclist won the Tour de France five times but only finished 12th in his sole appearance at the Games in 1964?

5 What was unique about the cycle race distances at the 1904 Games in St Louis?

6 When Jaime Huélamo and Aad van den Hoek were disqualified in 1972, why were their medals not awarded to the fourth-placed riders?

7 At which Games was an indoor velodrome used for all the track cycling events for the first time?

8 Which cycling event first contested at the Intercalated Games in 1906 was dropped from the schedule after the Munich Games, where the Soviet Union won their first gold medal in the competition?

9 Which cycling competition first appeared at the Games in 2000 and eight years later formed the second leg of Chris Hoy's gold medal treble?

"I shall be 53. To stay in the international-class shape is not that easy. Maybe I prefer to rest."

Jeannie Longo, ruling out a return from retirement to compete in an eighth Games

10 *Which nation has appeared in all but four editions of the Games since 1900 but had to wait until 2008 for its first cycling medal, gold for Juan Esteban Curuchet and Walter Fernando Pérez in the men's Madison?*

11 *Which legendary American cyclist competed in three editions of the Olympic Games and won only one medal, a bronze in the men's time trial in 2000?*

12 *Which cyclist was the first non-European to win the Tour de France but never competed in the Olympics, missing the Moscow Games because of the boycott and then turning professional before the 1984 edition?*

Answers:

1 Bicycle polo
2 Lotus
3 Professional cyclists were admitted
4 Eddy Merckx
5 They were all in imperial measurements
6 Because the fourth-placed riders had not undergone drugs tests
7 Montreal in 1976
8 Tandem
9 The keirin
10 Argentina
11 Lance Armstrong
12 Greg LeMond

IN THE WATER

By starting young in an Olympic sport that embraces so many different events, swimmers have been rewriting the record books almost at will. Ian Thorpe was the sensation in Sydney, and then along came Michael Phelps.

Such is their domination that it's sometimes easy to overlook the nine golds collected by Gary Hall Junior and Aleksandr Popov between them, the eight owned by Jenny Thompson, the four that are part of a collection of 12 for Dara Torres.

Further back, the achievements of Mark Spitz remain legendary, as do those of Don Schollander, who won seven golds at two Games. Gary Hall's dad wasn't bad either. And Kornelia Ender won three silvers at 13, four golds at 17 and nothing afterwards – a disturbing record for a teenager competing under the influence of East Germany's drug-fuelled desperation to succeed.

Water polo brings the excitement of head-to-head competition in the pool – although rather too dramatically when Hungary battled to gold in 1956. Diving delivers grace and agility and the occasional spectacular mishap. The synchronised disciplines will always either bedazzle or bemuse.

The aquatics events never stand still, with technology forever improving the timing, the pool infrastructure and the athletes' outfits. It's a far cry from the early days of open water when the participants would swim for gold – and for their lives.

20/12 Challenge

Warm-up Stretches

Swimming competitors at the 1896 Games were taken by boat into the Bay of Zea and left to swim back. The chilly April water took its toll and Alfréd Hajós of Hungary feared for his life but held on to take gold at 100m and 1,200m.

A 10km open water race was added to the men's and women's swimming schedules in Beijing. Maarten van der Weijden of the Netherlands won the men's race which came five years after his comeback in the sport following treatment for leukaemia.

Japan has won the most medals for synchronised swimming, with at least one in every Games since the event was introduced in 1984. But the total of 12 doesn't include any golds. Russia has only won six medals, but they are all gold.

Synchronised diving, which was introduced in 2000 for men and women, has been dominated by the Chinese, whose participants have won nine of the 12 gold medals awarded.

Michael Phelps became the youngest American male to swim at the Olympics for 68 years when he competed in Sydney in 2000. He then won six swimming gold medals at Athens in 2004 and followed up to claim eight more in Beijing in 2008.

"My will to live completely overcame my desire to win."

Alfréd Hajós of Hungary on completing a gruelling swimming challenge in the Bay of Piraeus in 1896

Among the swimmers whose achievements were eclipsed by Phelps was Mark Spitz. The American won two gold medals in 1968 in Mexico and seven more in 1972 in Munich, where he also set a new world record in each event.

Pat McCormick of the United States won the women's springboard and platform events in 1952 and 1956 to become the first diver to win four gold medals. Her compatriot Greg Louganis matched the feat in the men's events in 1984 and 1988.

American twins Karen and Sarah Josephson won the synchronised swimming duet in 1992, beating Canadian twins Penny and Vicky Vilagos in the final.

Hungary first entered the water polo competition in 1912 and soon began to dominate. The Hungarians took the silver medal in 1928 and then won four of the next five gold medals.

Ian Thorpe was only 17 when he won gold in the 400m freestyle on the first day of competition at Sydney in 2000. The Australian won two more golds in the relay events and took his total to five at the Athens Games in 2004.

East German swimmer Kristin Otto became the first woman to win six gold medals at the same Olympics. But her achievement in Seoul in 1988 is tarnished by allegations of a state-run performance-enhancing drugs programme.

Great Britain won four of the first five water polo tournaments but won nothing after the last gold in 1920 and has not entered the event since 1956.

Sammy Lee in 1952 became the first man to retain an Olympic platform diving title. After his retirement Lee worked with up-and-coming swimmers and coached Bob Webster, who became the second man to achieve back-to-back golds in 1960 and 1964.

Japan dominated the men's swimming event in 1932. Japanese swimmers took 11 of the 18 medals awarded including five out of six golds. They also demolished the 4x200m world record, beating it by 35 seconds.

Klaus Dibiasi had to settle for silver with second place in the platform competition in Tokyo. But the Italian won the event four years later and repeated the achievement in 1972 and 1976 to become the first diver to win three consecutive golds. Dibiasi also won a springboard silver in Mexico.

Manuel Estiarte was top scorer in each water polo tournament from 1980 until 1992 but without a medal to show for it until Spain lost the 1992 final to Italy in extra time. However, a first Spanish gold in 1996 more than compensated for him missing out for once on the scoring record.

Gary Hall Senior won four medals including one gold for the United States in an Olympic swimming career that lasted from 1968 until 1976. His son, Gary Hall Junior, took over from 1996 and went on to win 10 medals including five golds, with the last of them coming in 2004.

Jenny Thompson and Dara Torres each won 12 swimming medals for the United States. Thompson's career spanned four Games and included eight golds. Torres retired twice and missed the Games in 1996 and 2004 as a result, but she kept coming back and won three silvers in Beijing at the age of 41.

Australian swimming legend Dawn Fraser was denied the chance to extend her career by her own country's authorities. Fraser's record of eight medals included successive 100m golds from 1956 to 1964, but a ban imposed after allegations of misbehaviour at the Tokyo Games was lifted too late for her to prepare for Mexico.

Marjorie Gestring of the United States became the youngest known winner of any Olympic event with springboard gold in 1936 aged 13 years and 268 days. She failed to qualify for the next Games in 1948.

Race For The Line

1 *Which American who won five Olympic swimming golds and a water polo bronze in the 1920s subsequently embarked on an acting career, starring as Tarzan?*

2 *British swimmers Keri-Anne Payne and Cassandra Patten took silver and bronze respectively in the women's inaugural 10km swim in Beijing but for which nation did Larisa Ilchenko win gold?*

3 *What was permitted for swimmers from 1992 but was not taken up with any enthusiasm?*

4 *Which is the only nation to have won men's and women's water polo gold?*

5 *Which Australian won three women's swimming gold medals, one silver and one bronze at the 1972 Olympics in Munich and retired the following year aged 16?*

6 *Which nation won its first water polo medal in 1956, taking bronze in spite of offending opponents, officials and spectators with an angry reaction to defeat by Hungary?*

7 *Which American swimmer won a total of eight Olympic gold medals starting with one at Los Angeles in 1984 and concluding with two in Barcelona in 1992?*

8 *Which nickname was bestowed on Ian Thorpe after his swimming success?*

9 *For which nation did Matt Mitcham win the only diving gold medal in the 2008 men's and women's competitions that wasn't claimed by the Chinese hosts?*

> *"It teaches you to be patient when you are lying in a hospital bed and that was almost the same strategy I chose here, to wait for my chance in the pack."*

Leukaemia survivor Maarten van der Weijden of the Netherlands, after his endurance test at the 2008 Games

10　*Which team did Italy beat 20–18 in the 1996 water polo tournament to set a record aggregate score for the sport at the Games?*

11　*Which American swimmer denied Japan a clean sweep of the men's swimming medals in 1932 and later found fame as a TV and movie star in roles including Tarzan, Flash Gordon and Buck Rogers?*

12　*For which nation did Michelle Smith win three golds and a bronze in the pool at the 1996 Games?*

Answers:

1 Johnny Weissmuller
2 Russia
3 Two-piece costumes
4 Italy
5 Shane Gould
6 Soviet Union
7 Matt Biondi
8 Thorpedo
9 Australia
10 Hungary
11 Buster Crabbe
12 Ireland

ON THE WATER

Perhaps the biggest surprise from more than 100 years of Olympic events on the water is the dearth of reports of the competitors ending up actually in the water. A notable exception reportedly came in 1960 when Crown Prince Constantine was a member of the crew that won the Dragon class sailing for Greece and was given the traditional ducking by his mother, Queen Frederika.

Rowing and sailing have been part of the schedule for almost every edition of the Games since the start in 1896, and have produced some true champions in terms of medals won and some committed competitors with numbers of Games attended. The records set by Elisabeta Lipă and Steve Redgrave in rowing and by Hubert Raudaschl and Paul Elvstrøm in sailing may never be broken, but maybe people said the same years ago about Jack Beresford.

Kayak and Canadian events were introduced in the 1930s, and it is said the Pope watched some of the events from his summer palace when the Games went to Italy in 1960. The slalom was added more recently and has been dominated by teams from the Czech Republic and Slovakia, and by the Hochschorner brothers in particular.

But the outstanding participant on the water has been Birgit Fischer, whose achievements rank alongside the best in any Olympic competition.

20/12 Challenge

Warm-up Stretches

Hubert Raudaschl was the first Olympian in any sport
to compete in nine editions of the Games, and he nearly
achieved 10. The Austrian attended in 1960 but only as a
reserve. In 32 years of sailing competition from 1964 until
1996, he won silver in the Finn class in 1968 and in the
Star class 12 years later.

Paul Elvstrøm of Denmark competed in eight Games from
1948 until 1988 and became the first man in any sport to
achieve four consecutive wins in the same event. He took gold
at his first Games in the Firefly dinghy class and won the Finn
dinghy class in his next three appearances.

Birgit Fischer won 12 canoeing medals at six editions of the
Games between 1980 and 2004 – and would surely have
won more but for East Germany's boycott of Los Angeles in
1984. She won three golds and a silver during the 1980s and
continued after German reunification to win a further five
golds and three silvers.

Gert Fredriksson of Sweden came within 12 seconds
of securing a clean sweep of individual kayak medals
between 1948 and 1956. He won the 1,000m and 10,000m
events in London and in Melbourne and also took gold
in the 1,000m in Helsinki, but had to settle for second
there in the 10,000m.

"Every race we win is a motivation and when we keep winning it serves us in the future."

Pavol Hochschorner, who has won three successive Canadian slalom golds with his twin brother Peter

At the 1900 Games the Dutch coxed pair team picked a young boy from the crowd to replace cox Hermanus Brockmann, who was considered too heavy. The boy's age has since been estimated as between 7 and 10. It's possible he's the youngest Olympian ever, but nobody remembered to ask.

Canada was invited to demonstrate canoeing at the 1924 Games but proved out of its depth when the sport was added to the medal programme. After winning a handful of medals from their early attempts, the Canadians then went five Games without a canoeing medal.

Steve Redgrave won a record six rowing medals, five of them gold. The British rower won gold at every Games from 1984 to 2000 and added a bronze medal in 1988. He received a knighthood in 2001.

Jack Beresford won five rowing medals for Great Britain – including three golds – in an Olympic career that spanned five Games from 1920 until 1936. His achievement was a record in men's rowing until the arrival of Redgrave.

Elisabeta Lipă matched Redgrave's record of five golds with victory in the women's coxed eights in 2004. The Romanian also has two silvers and a bronze to her credit from six editions of the Games.

Vladimir Parfenovich in 1980 became the first man to claim three canoeing golds at the same Games, winning the individual kayak event at 500m and the pairs events at 500m and 1,000m.

Seven of the top eight women rowers in Olympic history are Romanian. Led by Lipă with her eight medals, the Romanians have three participants with a total of six medals and three more who have won five.

Torben Grael became the first man to win five Olympic sailing medals, with gold in the Star class at Athens in 2004. He had previously collected a gold and two bronze medals in the same event along with a silver in the Soling class in 1984.

Ben Ainslie of Great Britain set his sights on Paul Elvstrøm's record with four individual medals in consecutive Games. Ainslie won silver and then gold in the Laser class in 1996 and 2000 and moved to the larger Finn class to win gold in 2004 and 2008.

East Germany completed a clean sweep of all four gold medals when the canoe slalom was introduced to the Games schedule in 1972. But the event was then dropped from the programme and the country no longer existed by the time it was restored in 1992.

Two sets of brothers battled for rowing glory in the coxed pairs in 1992. Greg and Johnny Searle of Great Britain won the gold and ended the reign of the Italians Carmine and Guiseppe Abbagnale, who had won at the two previous Games.

Durward Knowles finished just outside the medals with Great Britain in the Star class in 1948. He then switched to represent the Bahamas at the next seven editions of the Games, winning bronze in 1956 and gold in 1964.

Twins Pavol and Peter Hochschorner became the first brothers to win canoeing gold when they finished first in the Canadian double slalom in 2000. The pair from Slovakia went on to retain their title in 2004 and 2008.

Disaster struck Denmark when their mast broke shortly before the start of the medal race in the 49er class in Beijing. Croatia, who had already been eliminated, came to the rescue and offered their boat as a replacement. Denmark sailed to the gold medal and then managed to navigate a series of protests from second-placed Spain.

In 1948 Róbert Zimonyi was the cox of the Hungarian boat that took bronze in the pairs. He moved to the United States after his country was invaded by the Soviet Union in 1956 and returned to the Games in 1964 to win gold for his adopted country in the eights.

Rowing is only denied a place among the ever-present Olympic sports because of the bad weather which forced the cancellation of the entire programme in 1896.

Race For The Line

1 *Which event was held once only, in 1908, attracted 17 participants from two nations and comprised three races of 40 nautical miles but produced only one finisher in each contest because of gale-force winds?*

2 *Torben Grael and his brother Lars, who won two bronze medals for sailing, were of Danish descent but helped make sailing the most successful Olympic event for which South American nation?*

3 *For which nation did Ian Ferguson win kayak singles, doubles and fours gold in 1984 followed by gold and silver in doubles events at the 1988 Games?*

4 *In which sailing competition did Alessandra Sensini of Italy and Barbara Kendall of New Zealand emerge as great rivals, winning seven medals between them following the event's introduction in 1992?*

5 *At which Games did Canada end its drought of five Olympic appearances without a canoeing medal?*

6 *Which British rower partnered Steve Redgrave to three gold medals and also won a fourth in 2004, after Redgrave's retirement?*

7 *Which sport with events including slalom and jumping featured in the Olympic programme just once, at the 1972 Games?*

8 *What nationality is Kathrin Boron, with four golds and a bronze the only non-Romanian in the top eight for women's Olympic rowing?*

"What separates the achievers is nothing as tangible as split times or kilograms. It is the iron in the mind, not the supplements, that wins medals."

Sir Steve Redgrave, after retiring from rowing and collecting his knighthood

9 *For which nation did Lee Lai-Shan win a first gold medal in the women's windsurfing event in Atlanta in 1996.*

10 *Who set records as the oldest and youngest woman to win canoeing gold medals at the Games?*

11 *What Olympic first did Sumner and Edgar White achieve when winning the 5.5m sailing class for the United States in 1952?*

12 *Which international sailing event did Russell Coutts of New Zealand win in 1995, 11 years after winning the Finn class at the Olympics?*

Answers:

1 Motor boating
2 Brazil
3 New Zealand
4 Windsurfing
5 1976 in Montreal
6 Matthew Pinsent
7 Waterskiing
8 German
9 Hong Kong
10 Birgit Fischer
11 Only twins to win sailing gold
12 The America's Cup

BALL CONTROL

The American version and the Aussie Rules option have made fleeting appearances at the Olympics and the Gaelic type will surely appear if the Games ever go to Galway, but Association Football was the first – and only lasting – format of the game on the schedule.

The meteoric success of football through various domestic leagues and high-profile international competitions has overshadowed and even threatened the Olympic competition, and the debate is at its most fierce in Great Britain, where the perhaps rhetorical question seems to be whether FIFA can be trusted to stick to its guarantees that the formation of a joint British side would not jeopardise the status of the four individual associations.

Certainly football at the Games has benefited from the appearance in recent years of some of the stars of the international game – Lionel Messi and Ronaldinho to name just two. But even they haven't had quite the impact of the United States basketball team of 1992. The Americans shouldn't need to wheel out such heavy artillery but history shows there have been occasions when they've underestimated the opposition at great cost, even in sports that they invented.

Hockey has also thrown up a few shocks, with India's dominance challenged, ended and now history. Maybe it's time to bring back cricket?

20/12 Challenge

Warm-up Stretches

Cricket appeared just once in the Games, in Paris in 1900. The Devon Wanderers touring side won the event for Great Britain, beating a French-based team comprised mainly of English expatriates – the only other team in the competition.

Great Britain has not entered a team into the Olympic football qualifying competition since 1972 and has not taken part at the Games itself since 1960, when they were eliminated in the group stage.

George Lyon, one of only five non-Americans among the 75 golfers who entered the 1904 tournament, became the only person from outside the United States to win a medal in the sport. The Canadian negotiated four rounds of matchplay and then beat Chandler Egan in the final.

Rechelle Hawkes of Australia is the most successful player in women's hockey at the Games. She is the only woman to have won three gold medals in the sport, having helped Australia to victory in 1988, 1996 and 2000.

Notwithstanding the occasional howler, the United States has dominated Olympic basketball. American Teresa Edwards also holds the record for the most medals, with four golds in her total of five gained between 1984 and 2000.

"The Football Associations of Scotland, Wales and Northern Ireland reiterate our collective opposition to Team GB participation at the 2012 Olympic Games."

Joint statement by those three football associations amid fears that formation of a joint British team for the Games would lead to the national sides being merged for other international tournaments

Canadian teams won the lacrosse tournaments on the two occasions that the sport featured in the programme. They beat the United States in 1904 and Great Britain in 1908.

Age restrictions for football at the Olympics explain the low count for individual medals. Eight women – all American – have each won three medals comprising two golds, along with only one man, Dezső Novák of Hungary.

Rugby union was contested at the Olympics from 1900 until 1924. The sevens version of the sport is due to return to the schedule from 2016.

Denmark became the only nation to win three consecutive gold medals for handball when they won the women's tournament in 2004. The Soviet Union and South Korea have each won two in a row but no nation has won consecutive titles in the men's event.

Hungary won a record third Olympic football gold medal in 1968, beating Bulgaria 4–1 in a bad-tempered final. The referee sent off three Bulgarians and one Hungarian.

India won the first of six consecutive hockey gold medals in 1928. They scored 29 goals in their five matches and didn't concede any.

The United States, founders of baseball, missed out on defending their Olympic title after failing to qualify for the 2004 tournament. The Americans flopped in the qualifying event 2–1 against Mexico, who subsequently lost 11–1 against Canada.

The United States women dominated the Olympic softball competition, winning the first three tournaments after the sport's introduction in 1996. But they were shock losers in the final in 2008, the last competition before softball was dropped from the Games.

Iraq's only attempt at Olympic basketball brought some of the heaviest defeats in the competition's history. In 1948 they were beaten 100–18 by Chile, 125–25 by China and 120–20 by South Korea. But somehow they still finished higher in the rankings than Ireland.

Uruguay won the Olympic football tournament in 1924 and in 1928 and never competed again, although the bulk of the 1928 squad stayed together to win the 1930 World Cup as hosts.

American football was played as a demonstration sport at the 1932 Games in Los Angeles. Aussie Rules featured as a demonstration sport in Melbourne in 1956.

The United States was cleared to select NBA players for the 1992 Games and made the most of the opportunity by lining up with some legends of basketball including Michael Jordan, Larry Bird, Charles Barkley and Earvin "Magic" Johnson.

Germany racked up some huge scores in dominating the 1936 handball tournament but only won three more medals after the sport returned to the men's schedule in 1972 – a gold for East Germany in 1980, silver for the West in 1984 and silver for the united Germany in 2004.

Denmark set an Olympic football scoring record in 1908 when they won 17–1 against the France 'A' side. Sophus Nielsen scored 10 of the goals.

Great Britain only squeezed into the 1984 men's hockey tournament as a late replacement for the boycotting Soviet team. They upset the form book by emerging unbeaten from the group stage and going on to win the bronze medal.

Race For The Line

1 *In addition to cricket which other traditional ball game was only contested in 1900, when the only competitors in two singles events and a doubles contest were French?*

2 *Which of the most dominant Olympic nations has never won a medal in men's or women's handball and stopped competing after 1996?*

3 *Women's basketball was added to the Games schedule in 1976. Which nation won the first two tournaments?*

4 *Which sport has been reinstated to the Olympic schedule for 2016 having not featured since 1904, when the United States won six medals to take their total to 10?*

5 *Which legendary Scottish football manager led the Great Britain team to fourth place at the Olympics in 1948?*

6 *Gennadi Volnov and Sergei Belov share the record for the most individual medals won in men's basketball. For which nation did they each win four medals, including one gold?*

7 *Which nation won the last Olympic rugby union tournament in 1924 and will therefore resume as reigning champions in 2016?*

8 *As the inaugural Premier League season was about to kick off there were no British-based players at the 1992 Games, but which future star of English football kept goal for the United States?*

9 *Which nation holds the record for the most Olympic gold medals in baseball, with three victories?*

"This group deserved gold. We knew coming in that we may never have this experience again."

Lionel Messi, football superstar and member of the Argentina team that won gold in 2008

10 *Which team was the first to beat India in an Olympic hockey match, with a 1–0 victory in the final in 1960?*

11 *At which sport did a world amateur team beat the United States in a demonstration event in 1936?*

12 *Which high-profile football referee whose appointments included the 2002 World Cup Final officiated in the 1996 Olympic final between Nigeria and Argentina?*

Answers:

1 Croquet
2 United States
3 Soviet Union
4 Golf
5 Matt Busby
6 Soviet Union
7 United States
8 Brad Friedel
9 Cuba
10 Pakistan
11 Baseball
12 Pierluigi Collina

TOUGH GUYS

It is said that boxers in the ancient Olympic Games wore leather straps on their hands and later added metal studs, and it's frightening to think what sort of damage such hard-hitters as Teófilo Stevenson might have inflicted with such equipment.

The advent of boxing gloves in time for the inclusion of the sport at the modern Games was therefore a welcome move, and there were other sensible innovations over the years. These included the admission of additional teams to prevent a repeat of the situation of 1904 when the Americans had to fight each other, and the practice of installing the referee inside the boxing ring rather than having him try to officiate from outside.

The most recent development is to open up Olympic boxing to women, something which happened years ago in martial arts, wrestling and weightlifting, and which helped produce such remarkable stories as Turkey's Nurcan Taylan hoisting twice her own body weight to win a gold medal and Ryoko Tamura winning judo medals at five successive Games.

Spare a thought though for Karen Briggs – best in the world at judo but injured at her first and only Olympics. And for Zbigniew Pietrzykowski. The Polish champion could have been a contender, but in two of his three Olympic challenges he came up against legends of the fight game in László Papp and Muhammad Ali.

Warm-up Stretches

*"Hey Floyd, I seen you!
Someday I'm gonna
whup you! Don't you
forget, I am the
greatest!"*

Cassius Clay, later to become
Muhammad Ali, as he won
Olympic gold in 1960 and set
his sights on beating world
heavyweight champion Floyd
Patterson

Angelo Parisi won a judo bronze for Great Britain at the 1972
Games but, after marrying a French woman, he went on
to win silver and gold in Moscow and another silver in Los
Angeles under the flag of his wife's nation.

Finland's Alfred Asikainen grappled with the Russian Martin
Klein for 11 hours and 40 minutes with only brief breaks in
the 1912 middleweight wrestling semi-final. Klein finally
won the longest bout ever recorded at the Games but was too
exhausted to compete in the final the next day.

At the same Games the light-heavyweight semi-final between
Ivar Böhling of Finland and Anders Ahlgren of Sweden
was abandoned as a draw after nine hours. Both men were
awarded a silver medal on the basis that neither had won.

Tough guys included girls when women's weightlifting
was added to the schedule in 2000, women's wrestling
in 2004 and women's boxing in 2012. Tara Nott of the
United States was the first gold medallist, winning
the 48kg weightlifting event in Sydney.

Kakhi Kakhiashvili won gold in weightlifting at
three consecutive Games and for two different
countries. Born in Georgia, he won the 90kg category
in 1992 as part of the Unified Team. He returned to
win gold at 99kg in Atlanta and at 94kg in Sydney,
each time representing Greece.

Héctor Rodríguez, who won judo gold at lightweight for
Cuba in 1976, said he only took up the sport to defend
himself against his six older brothers.

Brothers Yoshinobu and Yoshiyuki Miyake were only
separated by 7.5kg at the 1968 Games but it was enough for
Yoshinobu to take gold in the 60kg weightlifting category.
Yoshiyuki took bronze behind second-placed Soviet lifter
Dito Shanidze.

Tug of war was part of the athletics programme between 1900
and 1920. In 1908 the event was contested by British police
clubs, with City of London beating Liverpool in the final.

Japan has dominated judo at the Olympics but the first man
to win two gold medals was Dutch. Willem Ruska won the
heavyweight and open categories in Munich in 1972.

Hungarian boxing legend László Papp became the first man to win three successive gold medals in the ring when he beat Jose Torres of the United States in the 1956 light-middleweight final.

Eino Leino of Finland became the first wrestler to win medals in freestyle at four consecutive editions of the Games. Leino won gold at middleweight in 1920, silver at welterweight in 1924 and bronze at lightweight in 1928 and again at welterweight in 1932.

Viggo Jensen of Denmark and Launceston Elliot of Great Britain lifted the same weight in the two-handed event in 1896 but the Dane was declared the winner because Elliot moved his feet. The placings were reversed in the one-handed event.

Cassius Clay launched one of the greatest careers in sporting history when he won the 1960 light-heavyweight boxing gold medal in 1960. He later changed his name to Muhammad Ali, also called himself "The Greatest" and was nicknamed in the media as "The Louisville Lip".

Teófilo Stevenson arrived on the Olympic scene in explosive fashion to win heavyweight boxing gold in 1972. Stevenson went on to repeat his success in Montreal and Moscow and helped establish Cuba as a real force in the boxing ring.

With four World Championship titles and a Commonwealth Games gold medal to her name, Karen Briggs was one of the favourites when women's judo became a medal sport at the 1992 Games. But the British fighter's dreams were shattered when she dislocated her shoulder and couldn't finish her event.

Elmadi and Lucman Jabrailov went head-to-head in the 82kg wrestling programme in 1996 as brothers competing for different nations. Lucman was fighting for Moldova but it was Elmadi for Kazakhstan who progressed and finished fifth overall.

The British fighter Harry Mallin in 1924 became the first boxer to retain an Olympic title. Mallin beat his countryman John Elliott to win middleweight gold four years after his first success against the Canadian Georges Prud'Homme.

The addition of taekwondo to the full Olympic schedule in 2000 gave Vietnam the chance to win a first medal, silver for Tran Hieu Ngan in the women's 57kg event. The second came eight years later when Hoang Anh Tuan took silver in the men's 56kg weightlifting.

Born in Bulgaria, Naim Süleymanoğlu defected to Turkey and, although less than five feet tall, won weightlifting gold in 1988. He then retired but returned to become the first man to win weightlifting gold at three different Games with victories in 1992 and 1996.

Muhammad Ali's great boxing rivals Joe Frazier and George Foreman also won gold at the Olympics. Frazier won the heavyweight title in 1964 and Foreman emulated his success in 1968.

Race For The Line

1 *In which event did Rohullah Nikpai win Afghanistan's first Olympic medal – a bronze at the 2008 Games?*

2 *What nationality was Frank Kugler, who in 1904 became the first man to win medals in three different sports at the same Games in wrestling, weightlifting and tug of war?*

3 *Lennox Lewis won the World Heavyweight Championship for Great Britain but for which nation did he win Olympic boxing gold?*

4 *South Korea has dominated taekwondo at the Games but which nation edged them into second place in the medals table in 2004?*

5 *Soviet wrestler Aleksandr Karelin was unbeaten in international competition for 13 years, winning three Olympic gold medals and nine world championships. But at which Games did he have to settle for silver after finally losing to Rulon Gardner of the United States?*

6 *In which discontinued gym event did Viggo Jensen and Launceston Elliot also compete in 1896, finishing outside the medals?*

7 *For which nation did Félix Savón win three consecutive Olympic heavyweight boxing gold medals from 1992?*

8 *What nationality was Robert Van De Walle, who won gold in 1980, bronze in 1988 and in 1992 became the first judoka to appear in five Olympics?*

"I have never been hit so hard in all my 212 bouts."

West Germany's Peter Hussing after running into Cuban tough guy Teófilo Stevenson in the 1972 heavyweight boxing competition

9 *Cheryl Haworth of the United States tipped the scales at 300lbs to become the heaviest women's weightlifting medallist with bronze in 2000, but which other record did she set?*

10 *Which British boxer won the super-heavyweight boxing gold medal at Sydney in 2000?*

11 *In which event did the American Norbert Schemansky become the first man to win four medals, despite missing the 1956 Games through injury?*

12 *Which hard-hitting fighter won the Olympic super-heavyweight gold medal in 1996 prior to embarking on a successful professional career?*

Answers:

1 Taekwondo
2 American
3 Canada
4 Chinese Taipei
5 Sydney
6 Rope climbing
7 Cuba
8 Belgian
9 Youngest women's weightlifting medallist at 17 years
10 Audley Harrison
11 Weightlifting
12 Wladimir Klitschko

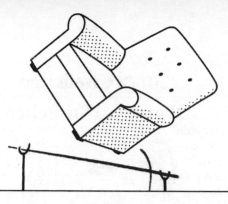

LEAPS AND BOUNDS

....

At its worst a curious concoction of ribbons and hoops, at its best a stunning combination of athleticism and aerobatics, gymnastics has been a staple of every Olympic Games in the modern era.

Perhaps surprisingly, given the physical demands on the participants, the sport has emerged relatively unscathed following the advent of drugs testing. Instead there has been greater suspicion around the age of the competitors – regulations adopted by the sport's governing body set the minimum age at 16 some time after Nadia Comăneci won gold as a 14-year-old.

The structure of the competition is such that a performer who has a good week can rewrite history by heading home with a clutch of medals. Among athletes in the more demanding sports, gymnasts are generally only bettered in terms of numbers of medals by swimmers, who are also able to target a glut of events.

Few gymnasts demonstrate the longevity of Takashi Ono, who won 13 medals for Japan across four editions of the Games. They tend to burn brightly on a couple of occasions or even cram all their success into a single Games.

For women, the trend is towards youth. Ágnes Keleti of Hungary won the last of her 10 medals in 1956, when pushing 36. Her great rival Larisa Latynina was nearly 22 when she won the first of her medals at the same Games. Twenty years or more later Nadia Comăneci and Olga Korbut had retired from the Games by the time they reached that age.

20/12 Challenge

Warm-up Stretches

Men had the gymnastics arena to themselves for 32 years as women were not allowed to compete until the 1928 Games in Amsterdam. Rhythmic gymnastics was added to the schedule in 1984.

Swimming sensation Michael Phelps took his overall medal tally to 16 in Beijing but Soviet gymnast Nikolay Andrianov still holds the record for most medals for men's individual events with 12 between 1972 and 1980.

Heikki Savolainen won his first gold at the age of 40 – 20 years after he first competed. The Finn had only bronze and silver for his efforts from 1928 to 1936 but took double gold in 1948 in the pommel horse and the team competition.

At just 14 years old Nadia Comăneci was one of the stars of the 1976 Olympics in Montreal and became the first gymnast to achieve a perfect score of 10.00, something she then repeated six times. The Romanian also won two gold medals in Moscow in 1980.

All of Ecaterina Szabo's gymnastics medals came in the 1984 Games in Los Angeles. With fellow Romanian Comăneci retired and the Eastern Bloc boycott removing serious Soviet competition, Szabo took gold in the individual vault, beam and floor competitions and the team competition plus silver in the all-around.

"Hard work has made it easy. That is my secret. That is why I win."

Nadia Comăneci, the Romanian who achieved gymnastics perfection at the age of just 14 in 1976

Věra Čáslavská started modestly with a team silver at the 1960 Games in Rome but went on to win seven individual gold medals – a record for a woman in any sport – during the Tokyo and Mexico City Games. She also added three more silver medals.

Gymnastics has produced the youngest known medallists for any sport. In 1896 Dimitrios Loundras of Greece finished third in the team parallel bars aged 10 years and 218 days. In 1928 Luigina Giavotti won silver with the Italian team at 11 years and 302 days.

Hermann Weingärtner's total of six gymnastic medals in 1896 helped Germany to a total of 10 and matched the haul of the entire Greek Olympic team. Weingärtner won gold for individual and team horizontal bars and in the team parallel bars. He took silver in the rings and pommel horse and bronze in the vault.

Sawao Kato of Japan won triple gold in 1968 and 1972 and finished off with two more in 1976. His total of eight golds is a record for men's gymnastics, but only five came in individual events compared with six for Nikolay Andrianov and Boris Shakhlin.

Alexander Dityatin became the only male gymnast to win medals in all eight events at the same Games when he lined up with the Soviet team in 1980. He won gold in the all-around and the rings to add to the team gold and then took four silver medals and one bronze.

Olga Korbut and Ludmila Tourischeva were team-mates and rivals at the 1972 Games. They both helped the Soviet Union win the team event before Korbut also claimed the beam and floor individual events, with Tourischeva victorious in the all-around.

Korbut and Tourischeva repeated their team success in Montreal but were upstaged by newcomer Nellie Kim, who twice achieved a score of 10.00 as she shared in the team triumph and also added individual golds for the floor and vault events.

China only entered the gymnastics from 1984 and after mixed fortunes over the years finished top of the medal table in Beijing with 18, including seven out of eight gold medals in the men's artistic events.

Dmitry Bilozerchev won three golds in 1988 but didn't have any to himself. In addition to his tied first place in the pommel horse, he was a member of the Soviet team that won gold and he came first in the rings – but tied again with Holger Behrendt of Germany.

Kerri Strug was hailed as the star of the seven-strong United States team in 1996 when she overcame an ankle injury to help them to first place in the all-around event which had been won by east European nations at the previous 12 Games.

All three finalists in the 1988 rhythmic all-around competition finished with a total of 40.00 after scoring a perfect 10.00 in each of their routines. However Marina Lobatch won the gold for the Soviet Union because she also achieved perfection in the preliminary routines which were used to settle the tie.

Soviet husband and wife Mikhail and Zinaida Voronin won eleven gymnastics medals between them at the 1968 Games in Mexico. With two gold, four silver and a bronze Mikhail missed out by one on the record that subsequently went to Alexander Dityatin. His wife won a gold, a silver and two bronze.

The men's pommel horse event produced a three-way tie in 1988 between Lyubomir Geraskov of Bulgaria, Zsolt Borkai of Hungary and Dmitry Bilozerchev of the Soviet Union. Forty years earlier another tie in the same event saw Heikki Savolainen share first place with fellow Finns Paavo Aaltonen and Veikko Huhtanen.

The Soviet Union didn't take part in the Olympics until 1952 in Helsinki and made an immediate impact on the gymnastics competitions. They finished top of the table with 22 medals, 11 each for the men and the women, and held the position at every Games in which they competed except two.

Vitaly Scherbo was the star when, after the break-up of the Soviet Union, a Unified Team claimed 20 gymnastics medals in 1992. The man from Belarus won six of their 10 gold medals in the parallel bars, vault, rings, pommel horse, all-round and the team event.

Race For The Line

1 *Which gymnastics event was added to the Olympic schedule in Sydney in 2000?*

2 *Which darling of the American media matched Ecaterina Szabo's feat of five gymnastics medals in 1984 but delivered only one gold?*

3 *Which music provided the backdrop to Věra Čáslavská's floor exercise routines in 1968, to the delight of the Mexican spectators?*

4 *Which woman gymnast set a record which still stands for all sports of 14 medals from individual events at the Olympics?*

5 *On which piece of apparatus did Alexander Dityatin become the first man to achieve a perfect 10.00 in 1980?*

6 *Which gymnast was variously nicknamed in the media as The Munchkin of Munich and The Sparrow of Minsk?*

7 *In which individual event did Nellie Kim and Nadia Comăneci tie for first place at the 1980 Games?*

8 *What was the nickname given to the United States women's team following their first ever gymnastics success in 1996?*

9 *Which nation denied China a clean sweep of men's gymnastics gold medals in Beijing by taking first place in the vault?*

10 *Karen Cockburn and Mathieu Turgeon won gymnastics medals for the first time in 16 years for which nation with a bronze each on the trampoline at Sydney?*

"Gymnastics uses every single part of your body, every little tiny muscle that you never even knew you had."

Shannon Miller, a member of the United States team that won a first gymnastics team gold in 1996

11 *Which nation took top spot in the gymnastics medals table in 1964 and 1968?*

12 *Who in 2008 became the first British competitor to win an individual gymnastics medal for 100 years when he took bronze in the pommel horse event?*

Answers:

1 Trampoline
2 Mary Lou Retton
3 The Mexican Hat Dance
4 Larisa Latynina
5 The vault
6 Olga Korbut
7 The floor
8 The Magnificent Seven
9 Poland
10 Canada
11 Japan
12 Louis Smith

HORSEPLAY

Germany's domination of equestrian events at the Games extends beyond the bare statistics displayed in various versions of the sport's medal table, which show Sweden not far behind.

Closer examination finds Reiner Klimke with six gold medals, Isabell Werth and Hans Günter Winkler with five each, Nicole Uphoff and Ludger Beerbaum with four each, alongside the best of the rest, Henri Saint Cyr of Sweden and the Dutch rider Charles Pahud de Mortanges.

Other nations can certainly match the Germans in terms of longevity; they just have fewer medals to show for their appearances at seven, eight or even nine editions of the Games. And if the Olympics are about taking part then no one should underestimate the achievements of Lorna Johnstone, a dressage competitor well past pensionable age, and Hiroshi Hoketsu, whose return to the Games in 2008 came 44 years after his only previous appearance.

With a solitary equestrian gold from 100 years of Olympic competition, Japan could be considered one of the sport's underachievers – as could China, who failed to make any impact on the competition even as hosts.

Olympic equestrianism has seen some of the events changed over the years, and women have been admitted and even allowed to compete on equal terms, but through it all Germany's superiority remains clear.

Warm-up Stretches

"I don't really feel any different. In our sport, youth is not necessarily an advantage and age and experience count for a lot."

Mark Todd, after coming out of retirement to return to Olympic equestrian action

Nurmi took gold in the three-day event in Berlin in 1936 – not the legendary Finnish distance runner but the mount of German rider Ludwig Stubbendorf.

Brothers Raimondo and Piero D'Inzeo took gold and silver respectively for Italy in show jumping at the 1960 Games and also set a record for Olympic appearances, reaching a total of eight in Montreal in 1976.

Women were admitted to equestrian events from 1952. Danish rider Lis Hartel, who was paralysed below the knee as a result of polio, was the first to win a medal in the individual dressage and repeated the success four years later.

Liselott Linsenhoff of West Germany won two medals at
the 1956 Games and became the first woman to win an
individual equestrian gold in 1972 when she won the
dressage event. Her daughter Ann-Kathrin won gold
in the team dressage in 1988.

Nicole Uphoff was the first woman to win four gold medals
in equestrian events. She won individual and team dressage
for West Germany in 1988 and the same events for the
united Germany four years later.

Polo was part of the programme for the 1900 Games and
also featured in four more editions before being dropped
after 1936. Great Britain won two golds outright and
claimed a third in a mixed team with the United States.

Show jumping was the first equestrian event to feature in
the Games programme. It first appeared in 1900 and
included a high jump competition, in which France
and Italy tied at 1.85m, and a long jump won by
Belgium with 6.1m.

Germans have won more equestrian medals than riders
from any other nation. In Berlin in 1936 Germany won
all six gold medals, the only clean sweep in the history
of the sport.

Swedish riders dominated the dressage competition in the
early 20th century, taking all three individual dressage
medals as hosts in 1912 and again in Antwerp in 1920.

In 1968, for the first time, no nation won more than one gold medal in equestrian events. Of the six nations who won one gold each, Great Britain edged out West Germany to take top spot in the medals table by virtue of having won two silvers.

Lorna Johnstone of Great Britain didn't win any medals but she became the oldest women to compete at the Games in any sport when she took part in the dressage in 1972 five days after her 70th birthday. She finished 12th.

The cross-country course in 1936 was so demanding that the four teams who managed to complete it all returned minus scores. Germany won with minus 676.65. Czechoslovakia finished fourth with minus 18,952.70.

The longest equestrian event in the history of the Games came in Stockholm in 1912 when the distance discipline required riders to cover 55km. Jean Cariou of France won that test on board Cocotte but their performance in the other disciplines brought only a bronze medal overall.

New Zealand had never won a medal in any equestrian discipline until Mark Todd took individual eventing gold in 1984. He repeated the achievement in 1988, adding a bronze in the team event, and emerged from retirement to win another bronze in 2000.

Arthur von Pongracz was 60 when he embarked on his Olympic career in the dressage events of 1924. He also competed in Amsterdam in 1928 and his last appearance came in Berlin in 1936 when, at the age of 72, he was a member of the Austrian team that finished fourth.

Andrew Hoy of Australia competed in six Games from 1984 and won gold in three consecutive team eventing competitions from 1992. He also took silver in the individual eventing competition in 2000.

Reiner Klimke switched from dressage to eventing and then back again before setting off in 1964 on a record-breaking run at the Games. The German won five team dressage golds, another for individual dressage and two individual bronze medals to achieve a total which remains unequalled in equestrian events.

Pierre Jonquères d'Oriola was the first rider to win the Olympic individual show jumping event twice – and 12 years separated his victories. The Frenchman took first place in Helsinki in 1952 and again in Tokyo, where he also won silver in the team event. He won a second silver in 1968.

Hans Günter Winkler won a record five Olympic show jumping gold medals, beginning with team and individual golds in 1956. He then won gold with the West German team in Rome, Tokyo and Munich, completing his collection with bronze in Mexico and silver in Montreal.

Michael Plumb waited for 16 years and was into his fifth Games before he won a first gold. Plumb won three consecutive silvers with the United States eventing team before they took gold in Montreal, where he also won silver in the individual event. The team missed out on defending their title in Moscow but won it again in Los Angeles.

Race For The Line

1 *Which Canadian rider has only won one medal – a silver for team jumping in 2008 – but at the same Games overhauled the appearance record of the D'Inzeo brothers by featuring in his ninth Olympics?*

2 *Which South American nation won its first equestrian gold medal in the 2004 Games, having collected bronze in 1996 and 2000?*

3 *What was achieved for the first time by the Czech rider František Ventura and his mount Eliot as they won gold in the individual jumping competition in 1928?*

4 *Which record-breaking German rider won dressage team gold with Liselott Linsenhoff in 1968 and again 20 years later with Linsenhoff's daughter Ann-Kathrin?*

5 *For which nation did Anky van Grunsven win a third consecutive individual dressage title at the 2008 Games?*

6 *Why was the team jumping competition declared void at Los Angeles in 1932?*

7 *Which nation in 2004 won the eventing individual gold for the first time since 1972?*

8 *Which rider won dressage gold at three separate Games on board Gigolo between 1992 and 2000 and collected gold again in 2008 riding Satchmo?*

9 *Which event sometimes referred to as gymnastics on horseback formed part of the equestrian schedule for the only time at the 1920 Games in Antwerp?*

"Hoketsu has been fighting for this dream for the last five years and his perseverance and attitude are admirable."

Trainer Ton de Ridder after Hiroshi Hoketsu qualified for the 2008 Olympics

10 *Hiroshi Hoketsu competed in show jumping in 1964 and returned to the Games in 2008 to take part in which other equestrian event, making him Japan's oldest ever Olympian at 67?*

11 *From which discipline were Sweden disqualified at the 1948 Games for breaking the rules by including a team member who was not a commissioned officer?*

12 *Where did the equestrian events take place at the 2008 Games?*

Answers:

1 Ian Millar
2 Brazil
3 No faults
4 Reiner Klimke
5 Netherlands
6 No team completed the course with three riders
7 Great Britain
8 Isabell Werth
9 Vaulting
10 Dressage
11 Dressage
12 Hong Kong

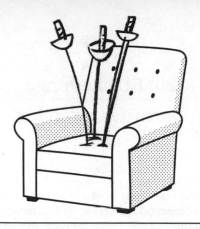

CHOOSE YOUR WEAPONS

Shooting, archery and even the more physically demanding fencing have produced some of the oldest Olympic medal winners, and none older than Oscar Swahn, who was 60 when he won his first gold medal in his debut Games. The First World War restricted his appearances to just two more editions of the Games.

The Swedish marksman eclipsed the record set in 1904 by Galen Spencer, a member of the victorious United States archery team at the age of 64 and two days. Spencer's countryman Samuel Duvall shot for the silver medal team at the age of 68 and 194 days.

In later years, as travel became less of a challenge, Olympians were able to set new longevity records at a relatively young age. Edoardo Mangiarotti and Aladár Gerevich fenced in five and six editions of the Games respectively, making their last appearances at 41 and 50, and would surely have competed in two more events but for the Second World War.

Ivan Osiier of Denmark competed in seven Games over 40 years, the last one in 1948 at the age of 59 and 240 days, making him the oldest Olympic fencer. He had a silver in 1912 to show for his efforts but other competitors were less fortunate. By 2008 Canadian shooter Susan Nattrass was at her sixth Games in 32 years. She had medals from the World Championships and the Commonwealth Games, but nothing from the Olympics.

20/12 Challenge

Warm-up Stretches

Shooting set a trend from 1896 when Georgios Orphanidis became the oldest competitor to win an event. The Greek came first in the free rifle competition at the age of 36 years and 102 days.

Oscar Swahn became the oldest gold medallist in any sport when he won the running deer shooting competition in 1912 at the age of 64 years and 257 days. The Swede also won a silver medal at the 1920 Games at the age of 72 years and 279 days, but he was too ill to compete in 1924.

Sybil "Queenie" Newall of Great Britain set the record as the oldest woman to win a medal in any sport when she won gold in the archery event in 1908. Newall's success came at the age of 53 years and 277 days.

Track and field athlete Neroli Fairhall competed in Paralympics events after she was injured in a motorcycle accident. But in 1984 she became the first paraplegic athlete to take part in the Olympics against able-bodied participants. Shooting from a wheelchair, the New Zealander came 35th out of 47 in women's archery.

Janice Romary never won an Olympic medal but in 1968 she became the first woman to compete in six consecutive editions of the Games. Romary first represented the United States in the foil competition at the 1948 Games at the age of 20.

"I have achieved the very best in sport. It's everything I could get."

Czech Republic sharp-shooter Kateřina Emmons, who won the first gold of the Beijing Games in the 10m air rifle competition

Shooting provided the first gold medal of the 2008 Games in Beijing. Kateřina Emmons of the Czech Republic achieved a perfect score in qualifying in the women's 10m air rifle competition and went on to equal the world record.

Born deaf, Ildiko Újlaky-Rejtő relied on written instructions from her coaches when she began fencing at the age of 15. She went on to represent Hungary in every Olympics from 1960 to 1976, winning gold, three silvers and a bronze in the foil team event plus a gold and a bronze in the individual competition.

Italy's Giovanna Trillini equalled the record of Újlaky-Rejtő of competing in five consecutive foil tournaments and beat her total of medals. She won four golds, a silver and two bronze between 1992 and 2004 before a bronze in Beijing gave her a total of eight.

British fencer Judy Guinness gave up her chance of a gold medal at Los Angeles in 1932 by telling judges after the final that they had failed to record two touches against her by Ellen Preis of Austria. Preis took gold, Guinness settled for silver.

As the only competing nation in 1904, hosts United States won 17 archery medals. It wasn't quite a clean sweep because they could only muster two squads for the women's team event so a bronze medal was not awarded.

Archery was dropped from the programme after 1920. When it returned in 1972, 24 years separated the gold medallists. John Williams won the men's gold at the age of 18 and the women's title went to fellow American, 42-year-old Doreen Wilber.

Margaret Murdock in 1976 became the first woman to win an Olympic shooting medal – and it could have been gold. Murdock tied for first place with United States team-mate Lanny Bassham but was relegated to second after comparison of the last 10 shots. Rules forbade a shoot-off but Bassham insisted Murdock share top spot on the podium.

The United States dominated the 1904 Games as hosts but Cuba cleaned up in the fencing. Ramón Fonst won gold in the foil and the epee, Manuel Díaz took gold in the sabre and the pair combined with American Albertson Van Zo Post to win the team foil.

South Korea didn't win its first archery gold until 1984 when Seo Hyang-Soon took gold in the women's individual event. But as hosts the Koreans won three out of four golds in 1988, missing out only on the men's individual title when for the first time the competition featured team events.

In 1992 China's Zhang Shan became the first woman to win a mixed shooting event in the skeet competition. She was also the last, as mixed shooting events have not been held since.

Edoardo Mangiarotti won a record 13 medals for Italy in epee and foil events beginning with gold in Berlin in 1936 and concluding with gold and silver in Rome in 1960. His total included six golds and five silvers.

The achievement of Aladár Gerevich of winning six golds in the same event remains a record for any sport. Gerevich won a total of 10 medals including team sabre for Hungary for six consecutive Games from 1932. In common with Mangiarotti, his achievements would have been even greater but for the interruption of the Second World War.

Brothers Nedo and Aldo Nadi of Italy became the first fencers to win gold with all three weapons at the same Games. Nedo won five golds at Antwerp in 1920 to add to his individual foil gold from the 1912 Games. Aldo won gold in the three team events in 1920 and silver in the individual sabre.

Great Britain won five archery medals as London hosted the Games in 1908 but had to wait 80 years for the next success in the sport, with bronze in the men's team competition in 1988.

American marksman Lloyd Spooner set a record for any Olympic sport by competing in 12 events at the same Games in 1920. The United States won 23 shooting medals and Spooner helped deliver seven of them, with four golds, a silver and a bronze in the team competitions plus an individual bronze.

Race For The Line

1 *Which Swedish fencer who also never won a medal overtook Janice Romary's record in 1988 and finished with appearances at seven Olympics?*

2 *Which nation won 20 archery medals including 11 golds between 1900 and 1920 but failed to win any after the sport returned to the Games schedule in 1972?*

3 *South Korea won three out of four archery gold medals in 2000 and 2004. Which European nation denied them a clean sweep by winning the men's individual event in 2004?*

4 *What was significant about Xu Haifeng's gold medal in the men's 50m pistol competition in 1984?*

5 *Which nation and former Games host has competed in the most Olympic archery competitions without winning a medal, with nine attempts?*

6 *Which is the only nation to have won a women's fencing medal at every Games since 1980?*

7 *Which former Soviet state in 2008 won its first archery gold medal since its independence in 1991?*

8 *Walter Winans won double gold for the United States. He won the running deer shooting class in 1908 and which event in the inaugural Olympic art competition in 1912?*

9 *Which European nation considered by some to be the birthplace of fencing didn't win its first Olympic medal in the sport until 2008?*

> *"It was not an act of defiance but a personal thing. There was no way she deserved to stand lower while the national anthem was played."*

Lanny Bassham after sharing the podium with Margaret Murdock in 1976

10 *Which former European nation competed in 1992 under the banner of Independent Olympic Participants and won just three medals, all in shooting?*

11 *Which nation won all three medals in the women's individual sabre event in Beijing but could only manage bronze when the three participants joined forces for the team event?*

12 *Which husband and wife team won shooting medals at the 2004 and 2008 Olympics, but each for different nations?*

Answers:

1   Kerstin Palm
2   Belgium
3   Italy
4   It was China's first gold in any sport
5   Canada
6   Italy
7   Ukraine
8   Sculpture
9   Spain
10 Yugoslavia
11 United States
12 Matthew and Katerina Emmons for the United States and
    the Czech Republic

NET WINNERS

French players partnered with Americans, Americans joined forces with British players, British players teamed up with the French and one of them even won the doubles with a German. Such was the scenario in Olympic tennis, confusing the medal count until 1904, when the Americans basically kept the tournament to themselves.

Things became more stable after that but only until 1924, when the event was scrapped. Its absence denied some legends of the game the chance to add Olympic gold to Grand Slam glory, but since 1988 the competition has attracted some of the best players in the world.

Volleyball was another opportunity for the Americans and the Soviets to flex their sporting muscles when it appeared on the scene during the 1960s but it also provided Brazil with a chance to make their mark at the Games, particularly following the introduction of beach volleyball. Only sailing has brought more success for the hosts of 2016.

Victory for any non-Asian country is rare on the badminton court, and no one comes close to China in the medals list for table tennis. Western nations celebrate the occasional success but the record in Beijing of one European table tennis medal compared to eight for the hosts tells its own story.

20/12 Challenge

Warm-up Stretches

The decline of British tennis is demonstrated by the respective medal counts before and after the exclusion of the sport from the Olympics. Between 1896 and 1924 Great Britain sat atop the medal table with around 40, including 15 gold. Since the event was restored in 1988 Great Britain has won one silver.

The United States was the first nation to make a clean sweep of tennis medals. They won everything in the men's singles and doubles in St Louis in 1904 but were assisted by the fact that more than 30 competitors included only one non-American.

John Boland won gold for Great Britain in the men's singles in the first tennis tournament in 1896 and partnered with the German Friedrich Traun to also win the men's doubles.

Great Britain won all four gold medals in 1900 as the Doherty brothers dominated. Lawrence won the singles with Reginald taking bronze and they teamed up to take the doubles. Reginald joined Charlotte Cooper to win the mixed doubles. Great Britain peaked by winning 15 of 18 medals in London in 1908.

Badminton made its debut as a medal sport in 1992 and was dominated from the start by Asian nations. Pairs from South Korea won the men's and women's doubles events and the singles competitions were both won by Indonesia.

"They are not even Georgians!"

Russian beach volleyball player Alexandra Shiryayeva after losing at the 2008 Games to bitter rivals Georgia, whose team comprised two imports from Brazil

Norris Williams, who survived the sinking of the Titanic and resisted suggestions from a doctor that his legs be amputated because they were so badly damaged by the cold, recovered to play in the 1924 tennis tournament. He won the mixed doubles with fellow American Hazel Wightman.

Japan progressed from men's volleyball bronze in 1964 to silver in 1968 and finally won gold in 1972 but their players haven't won a medal in the men's event since.

At the age of 43, Winifred McNair became the oldest women's doubles tennis champion and the oldest British woman to win gold in any sport when she partnered Kathleen McKane – 19 years her junior – to success at the 1920 Games in Antwerp.

Full, six-a-side volleyball was introduced to the men's and women's schedules as a medal sport in 1964. Beach volleyball, with teams of two, was added as a demonstration sport in 1992 and as a medal event four years later.

The Soviet Union and Russia won a volleyball medal at every Games they entered except 1996 when the men's and women's teams both lost their play-offs for bronze.

As war broke out between Russia and Georgia in August 2008, the two nations met in the women's beach volleyball at the Beijing Olympics. Defeat for Russia removed any hope of advancing to the knockout stage and proved particularly frustrating because the victorious Georgians were both born in Brazil.

Tennis appeared as a demonstration sport in 1968 and again in 1984 when Sweden's Stefan Edberg beat a field that included Guy Forget and Pat Cash. Steffi Graf won a women's tournament that featured Andrea Jaeger and Kathy Horvath.

Cuba caught up with the rest of the world in women's volleyball by winning their first gold in Barcelona in 1992. They also took gold in 1996 and 2000 and Regla Torres and Mireya Luis featured in all three teams.

Deng Yaping won four table tennis gold medals for China in 1992 and 1996. She won the women's doubles on both occasions with Qiao Hong and in 1992 won the singles final against her partner.

Table tennis never featured at the Games as a demonstration sport but appeared as a medal sport for men and women from 1988. It has been dominated by China ever since, with 20 of the 24 gold medals contested.

Tennis superstar Andre Agassi won the men's singles final at the 1996 Games. His success came nearly 50 years after his father Emmanuel Aghassian had made the family's Olympics debut for Iran in the boxing ring in 1948.

Nicolás Massú became the first man since tennis returned to the Games to win the singles and doubles in the same year. He beat Mardy Fish in the singles final in 2004 and partnered with Fernando González to win the doubles as Chile dominated the event.

China didn't compete at badminton when the sport appeared as a demonstration event at the 1972 Games but their players took five medals in 1992 and have dominated the event ever since.

Only Indonesia stood between China and a clean sweep of badminton gold medals in Sydney in 2000. China won the men's and women's singles and the women's and mixed doubles, but Tony Gunawan and Candra Wijaya took gold in the men's doubles.

Boris Becker and Roger Federer racked up the Grand Slam wins in singles events but only won Olympic gold in the doubles. Becker partnered Michael Stich to victory in 1992 and Federer won with Stanislas Wawrinka in 2008.

Race For The Line

1 *Who partnered Neil Broad to win silver for Great Britain in the men's tennis doubles at Atlanta in 1996?*

2 *Which nation did Hugo Hardy represent when he lost his singles and doubles matches as the only foreigner in the tennis tournament in St Louis in 1904?*

3 *Brothers Razif and Jalani Sidek won a first medal for which nation with bronze in the men's badminton doubles in 1992?*

4 *Apart from China, which is the only nation to have achieved double figures in terms of medals won for table tennis?*

5 *Which future Grand Slam champion became the youngest player to win an Olympic tennis medal when she won the women's singles in Barcelona at the age of 16?*

6 *Winthrop "Wink" Davenport was a member of the United States team that competed in the 1968 volleyball tournament. In which event did his daughter win gold in 1996?*

7 *Which was the first European nation to win a medal for badminton after the sport was added to the full Olympic programme with a bronze in 1992?*

8 *Which nation competed in the Games for the first time in 1920 but had to wait until 1996 for its first women's gold medal courtesy of beach volleyball champions Jackie Silva and Sandra Pires?*

9 *Which is the only landlocked nation to have won a medal in beach volleyball?*

"The ultimate boast is Olympic gold."

Serial Grand Slam-winner Venus Williams after collecting her third Olympic tennis gold in 2008

10 *Which is the only European nation to have won a gold medal in table tennis?*

11 *Which European nation can equal Brazil and the United States with four medals for men's volleyball but has never won gold?*

12 *Which is the only nation to have won a gold medal for badminton at every Games since the event became a medal sport in 1992?*

Answers:

1 Tim Henman
2 Germany
3 Malaysia
4 South Korea
5 Jennifer Capriati
6 Lindsay Davenport won the women's tennis singles
7 Denmark
8 Brazil
9 Switzerland
10 Sweden
11 Italy
12 Indonesia

ALL-ROUNDERS

If Robert Garrett wasn't the inspiration for the "athlons" then he should have been. The pentathlon and decathlon for men didn't come along until 1912, and even the "ancient" pentathlon of the Intercalated Games arrived after Garrett's remarkable achievements.

The American's failure in the discus competition in 1900 stood out because it was the only one of seven events across two editions of the Games in which he didn't win a medal. In 1896 Garrett won the discus and shot competitions and took silver in the long jump and high jump, with three of the events taking place over the same two days. Four years later he took bronze in the shot and in the standing triple jump.

Other Olympians have tackled different events related to their stronger sports. Irena Szewińska and particularly Carl Lewis competed successfully on the track and in the long jump, and Fanny Blankers-Koen tried field events before committing to a glittering sprint career.

But the true all-rounders are recognised to be those who test themselves over a number of different disciplines in two strenuous days of competition, and who also face the mental calculation referred to by Daley Thompson – deciding whether it will be enough to concentrate on their strengths or whether the priority is to prevent opponents from exploiting weaknesses.

Warm-up Stretches

The men's all-around athletics competition – a forerunner of the decathlon – was one of only two track and field events at St Louis in 1904 to be won by a non-American. Tom Kiely, an Irishman running under the flag of Great Britain, took first place.

The pentathlon and the decathlon were introduced for men at the 1912 Games in Stockholm and Jim Thorpe won them both. He also came fourth in the high jump and seventh in the long jump, so competed in a total of 17 athletics competitions.

At 17, Bob Mathias of the United States was considered too young to be a serious contender for decathlon gold at London in 1948. But he won the competition and four years later became the first participant to achieve double success in the event.

The modern pentathlon combination of fencing, shooting, swimming, show jumping and running proved particularly popular with Sweden, which won eight of the first nine individual gold medals including clean sweeps in the first three events.

Daley Thompson competed in his first Olympic decathlon for Great Britain in 1976, finishing 18th on his 18th birthday. He won the event in 1980 and 1984 to become the first man since Bob Mathias to retain the title.

"Thanks, King."

Jim Thorpe's reply to King Gustav V of Sweden, who congratulated the American after his success in 1912 and hailed him as "the greatest athlete in the world"

If the 1932 schedule had included multiple events for women, Mildred "Babe" Didrikson Zaharias would have taken some catching. The American won gold in the 80m hurdles and the javelin and silver in the high jump. In domestic sport she was prominent in baseball and basketball, and she became an internationally-renowned golfer.

András Balczó was the first man to win three gold medals in the modern pentathlon. He was a member of the victorious Hungary team in 1960 and 1968 and also won the individual event in 1972. Pavel Lednyov of the Soviet Union holds the record for the most medals in the event, with seven – including two golds – between 1968 and 1980.

The women's pentathlon, which was replaced by the heptathlon in 1984, ran for five editions of the Games and produced clean sweeps of the medals for East Germany in 1976 and the Soviet Union in 1980.

Peter Macken set a modern pentathlon record by competing in the event at five successive Games from 1960. The Australian also took part in the team fencing competition in Mexico. He didn't win any medals but finished fourth in his main event in 1964.

Carolina Klüft of Sweden turned her back on the heptathlon after winning gold in Athens in 2004 and said she would concentrate on long jump and triple jump. She entered both events in Beijing but finished well outside the medal positions.

The triathlon was introduced for men and women in 2000. No individual has ever won it twice but Simon Whitfield won gold in 2000 and silver in 2008 for Canada and Bevan Docherty won silver in 2004 and bronze in 2008 for New Zealand.

The United States dominated the decathlon with six straight gold medals from 1932 to 1960 and are the only nation to achieve a clean sweep of the medals, first in 1936 and then in 1952.

Sheila Taormina became the first woman to compete in three different sports. She won gold for the United States in the 4x200m freestyle relay in 1996 but couldn't win a medal in the triathlon competitions of 2000 or 2004 or the modern pentathlon in 2008.

The men's pentathlon was dropped from the schedule after its third appearance in 1924. Finland's Eero Lehtonen retained the gold medal won at the 1920 Games. He competed less successfully in the long jump and decathlon in 1920 and in the 4x400m in 1924.

Andrey Moiseyev of Russia in 2008 became the first man to win back-to-back individual gold medals in the modern pentathlon since Lars Hall, who completed the achievement for Sweden in 1956.

Jackie Joyner-Kersee in 1992 became the only woman to win the heptathlon twice – and it could have been more. The American came within five points of gold in the inaugural event in 1984, ironically after struggling in the long jump – an event in which she would later win gold and bronze individual medals.

In an event dominated first by the United States and more recently by European nations, the achievements of C.K. Yang from Chinese Taipei are remarkable. A student at UCLA, Yang challenged in the high jump and the decathlon in 1956 and won decathlon silver in 1960. He came fifth defending his title in 1964, when he also competed in the pole vault.

Five people have won medals at the Summer and Winter Olympics but only four have won them in summer and winter events. Gillis Grafström of Sweden collected four medals in winter sports, but his first gold came when skating formed part of the programme at the 1920 Summer Games.

The pace of Morris Kirksey helped the United States win rugby union gold in 1920. By the time the Americans beat France to take the title, Kirksey had already won gold in the 4x100m relay and silver in the individual 100m.

London-born Teddy Flack emigrated as a child and so won the 800m and the 1,500m in 1896 as Australia's first Olympian. But in the tennis he partnered George Robertson of Great Britain to take bronze in the men's doubles.

Race For The Line

1 *A United States competitor of mixed ancestry, what was the English translation of Jim Thorpe's Native American name?*

2 *Which nation has won four of the nine women's triathlon medals to be awarded, including gold and bronze respectively for Emma Snowsill and Emma Moffatt in 2008?*

3 *Lottie Dod – a five-time Wimbledon ladies' singles champion – retired from competitive tennis in the 1890s and also excelled at golf and hockey. But in which event did she win Olympic silver in 1908?*

4 *Which is the only nation outside Europe to have won any medals in the modern pentathlon?*

5 *Which sport did Daley Thompson play professionally, briefly, after retiring from athletics?*

6 *Which Middle East nation claimed its only Olympic gold medal courtesy of Ghada Shouaa's victory in the heptathlon in 1996?*

7 *Which is the only nation to have won gold, silver and bronze medals in the women's modern pentathlon?*

8 *Denise Lewis in 2000 became the first British woman to win a multi-discipline athletics event since which winner of the pentathlon in 1972?*

9 *In which year did Glynis Nunn of Australia win heptathlon gold before missing out on the medals in the individual long jump and 100m hurdles events?*

"Sometimes you have to resist working on your strengths in favour of your weaknesses. The decathlon requires a wide range of skills."

Double-Olympic champion Daley Thompson on his preparations for the decathlon

10 *Which athlete who missed out controversially on qualification for the 1992 decathlon delivered a first United States gold in the event for 20 years when he appeared in 1996?*

11 *In which event did Great Britain's Mary Rand win a silver medal in 1964 to go with her gold in the long jump and bronze in the 4x100m?*

12 *For which European nation did Helge Løvland win a one-and-only decathlon medal when he took gold in 1920?*

Answers:

1 Bright Path
2 Australia
3 Archery
4 United States
5 Football
6 Syria
7 Great Britain
8 Mary Peters
9 1984
10 Dan O'Brien
11 Pentathlon
12 Norway

LEGENDS

If winning an Olympic gold medal is one of the greatest achievements in sport, what price winning two? Or three? Or 14?

And how do you compare the high-intensity performance of someone who collected their medals over a few days with the ongoing effort of a specialist who made an event their own over a period of 20 years or more?

Then there are the athletes who found popular support from their failure for one reason or another to turn global domination of a particular discipline into Olympic medals – loss of form, injury, political boycotts and even war getting in the way of a bid for glory.

When it comes to building the profile of an Olympic legend, there is no doubt that live and increasingly sophisticated media coverage gives the stars of the modern age an advantage over their rivals from any Olympic Games – for Paavo Nurmi, TV punditry just wasn't an option.

The evidence is also clear that certain events produce more multiple medal winners than others, with swimmers and gymnasts particularly prolific. One or two rowers have notably won several as well, but Steve Redgrave was entitled to let his achievements speak for themselves when he was advised by one wise guy to "try a sport where you don't get to sit down."

20/12 Challenge

Warm-up Stretches

Carl Schumann was the first multiple gold medal winner in
the modern Olympic age. At Athens in 1896 he entered 12
events, won individual gold in the vault and team gold with
Germany in the parallel bars and horizontal bars. His fourth
gold was for wrestling.

Michael Phelps became the youngest American male to swim
at the Olympics for 68 years when he competed in Sydney
in 2000. Perhaps the most remarkable aspect of his success
is that it has all come at just two editions of the Games, and
there is time for him to achieve much more.

Before Phelps, the most successful swimmer in Olympic
history was Mark Spitz. Events of 2004 and 2008 show
the American's achievements of 1968 and 1972 are now
vulnerable, but they stood unchallenged for 36 years.

Larisa Latynina from the Soviet Union dominated women's
gymnastics between 1956 and 1964. She won four gold medals
in Melbourne, three in Rome and two in Tokyo. Her total of
nine remains a record for a gymnast and for a woman.

Jumping events featured a "standing start" version when Ray
Ewry won his 10 Olympic gold medals between 1900 and
1908. The American won four successive standing high jump
and standing long jump events and also won the standing
triple jump in 1900 and 1904.

"I hereby give permission to anybody who catches me in a boat again to shoot me."

Steve Redgrave in 1996, before changing his mind and returning to the Olympics to win a fifth gold in Sydney in 2000

Paavo Nurmi was the first Olympian to win nine gold medals. Five came in Paris in 1924 when the Finn won the individual 1,500m, 5,000m and cross-country events as well as the team cross-country and 3,000m events.

The lightning pace of Carl Lewis brought him nine Olympic gold medals between 1984 and 1996. In addition to four successive long jump golds, the American won the sprint double of 100m and 200m in Los Angeles in 1984, the 100m in Seoul in 1988 and the sprint relays in Los Angeles and Barcelona in 1992.

Nikolay Andrianov became the most decorated male gymnast with his achievements between 1972 and 1980. Of his 15 medals, which included seven gold, the Soviet star claimed 12 from individual events rather than from team competitions.

The Games almost came too late for Oscar Swahn. The Swede was 60 when he contested his first shooting events in London in 1908 but he won two golds and a bronze and would contest two more editions of the Games and take three more medals before retiring as the oldest medal winner.

The Lafortune family from Leuven in Belgium illustrate perfectly that "the most important thing in life is not the triumph but the struggle." François Lafortune Senior, his brother Marcel and his son François Junior appeared in 16 Olympic shooting competitions between them from 1924 until 1976 without a winning a medal.

Olympic boxing still provides one of the best opportunities to witness the rising stars, hungry for their shot at glory. Many have gone on to win world titles, with Muhammad Ali the prime example. But Teófilo Stevenson reached TV audiences worldwide to deliver prime-time punching over three successive Games.

Jamaican-born sprinter Merlene Ottey never won Olympic gold but competed in every Games between Moscow in 1980 and Athens in 2004, collecting three silvers and six bronzes. Aged 48, she narrowly missed out on qualifying to represent her adopted country, Slovenia, at Beijing in 2008.

When it comes to team games, the United States basketball players deliver value all the way. Their victories are always routine, their defeats always crushing. Their response to catastrophe in 1988 was spectacular – a who's who of the NBA averaged 117 points a game in 1992 and the tightest margin of victory was 32.

Fanny Blankers-Koen became the first woman to win four athletics gold medals at the same Olympics in London in 1948. She had made her Games debut in 1936 and returned after the break for the Second World War to win the 80m hurdles, the 100m, 200m and the sprint relay.

Steve Redgrave announced his retirement after winning a fourth successive rowing gold for Great Britain at the 1996 Olympics in Atlanta but he was back in action four years later to take his total of gold medals to five with victory in Sydney.

Aladár Gerevich won seven gold medals in six Olympic Games spanning 28 years which included the Second World War. The Hungarian fencer won six of his medals in the sabre team event and one as an individual, starting at Los Angeles in 1932 and bowing out after Rome in 1960.

Birgit Fischer's eight gold medals came from six Games in 24 years. The German became the youngest Olympic kayaking champion in Moscow in 1980 and won her last medals – a gold and a sliver in Athens in 2004 – as the oldest.

World records tumbled when Usain Bolt took to the track in Beijing in 2008. The Jamaican became the first man to break the world record in winning the 100m and 200m and he made it a hat-trick when his team produced another record-breaking run in the sprint relay.

Al Oerter was the first track and field athlete to win four consecutive Olympic gold medals in the same individual event. The American also set a new Olympic record in winning the men's discus in Montreal in 1956 and at the next three Games in Rome, Tokyo and Mexico.

Jesse Owens was the sensation of the 1936 Olympics in Berlin. The African-American defied Adolf Hitler's theory of Aryan superiority by winning gold in the 100m, 200m, 4x100m relay and the long jump, setting two world records in the process.

Race For The Line

1 *How many of his 14 Olympic gold medals did Michael Phelps win for individual events as opposed to relay events?*

2 *At which Games did Bradley Wiggins win the first of his six Olympic cycling medals?*

3 *For which nation did Věra Čáslavská win seven gold medals in gymnastics, including four in Mexico in 1968?*

4 *Which boxer won Olympic gold at light-welterweight in 1976 and subsequently embarked on a professional career that brought victories over such legendary fighters as Marvin Hagler, Roberto Durán and Thomas Hearns?*

5 *In which event did Usain Bolt compete at the 2004 Olympics?*

6 *Who was the only member of the United States basketball "Dream Team" to start all of their matches in 1992?*

7 *Which distance runner ended the hopes of his compatriot Haile Gebrselassie of a third 10,000m gold by winning the event in 2004 and 2008, when he also took the 5,000m title?*

8 *At which Olympics did Steve Redgrave win his only bronze medal for rowing?*

9 *In which field event did Fanny Blankers-Koen compete for the Netherlands at the 1936 Olympics in Berlin?*

10 *What was the nickname given to Liu Xiang, who left the Chinese nation distraught when he was forced to pull out of the 110m hurdles on home soil?*

"After I came home from the 1936 Olympics with my four medals, it became increasingly apparent that everyone was going to slap me on the back, want to shake my hand or have me up to their suite. But no one was going to offer me a job."

Jesse Owens

11 *Which African athlete ignored medical advice and overcame a gallbladder infection to win the 1,500m and take silver in the 5,000m in Mexico in 1968?*

12 *Which legend of the English Premier League scored the only goal when Argentina beat Paraguay to win the 2004 Olympic football final?*

Answers:

1 Nine
2 Sydney
3 Czechoslovakia
4 Sugar Ray Leonard
5 200m
6 Michael Jordan
7 Kenenisa Bekele
8 Seoul in 1988
9 The high jump
10 Shangai Express
11 Kip Keino
12 Carlos Tevez

OLYMPIC ODDMENTS

So many records, so many stats, so many stories. And there are more. It is said that Forrest Smithson, an American student of theology, carried a bible when he broke the world record for the 110m hurdles in 1908, that a French sprinter in 1896 wore gloves out of respect for the royal audience and that Billy Sherring donned a trilby when he ran to the gold medal in the marathon at the Intercalated Games. And was presented with a goat.

When Paavo Nurmi fell into the water during the 3,000m steeplechase heats in 1928 he was helped to his feet by Lucien Duquesne, and then ran as a pacemaker to help the Frenchman join him in the final. Sohn Kee-Chung, a Korean, won the 1936 marathon under the Japanese flag but refused to acknowledge the anthem. At the age of 76, he carried the Olympic torch with pride when the Games arrived in Seoul. In Beijing, Fu Yiquan joined the ranks of Games volunteers at the age of 103.

Then there are tales of athletes tugging shirts and taking illegal substances. Tom Hicks, running in the marathon in 1904, was found to have taken strychnine as a stimulant. But that was not illegal at the time and although Hicks crossed the line in second place, he won gold because Fred Lorz was the marathon runner who hitched a lift.

But rather than dwell on the con men and criminals, here's a round-up of the customs, the curious and the quirky.

20/12 Challenge

Warm-up Stretches

Medal ceremonies were introduced at the Los Angeles Games in 1928. Prior to that the medals were awarded as part of the closing ceremony.

John Boland, who won two gold medals for tennis at the first Games in 1896, initially had no intention of competing in any events and was only in Athens to visit a friend for Easter.

Greta Andersen of Denmark won the women's 100m freestyle gold medal in 1948 and 16 years later set the female record for swimming the English Channel.

Bob Mathias, the first man to win the decathlon twice, embarked on a TV and movie career after his retirement from athletics in 1952 and also served the state of California as a United States congressman.

Daniel Carroll set a record as the youngest winner of a rugby union gold medal when he struck gold with the Australasia team in 1908. In 1920 he won the competition again, this time with the United States team.

The first basketball victory for the United States after the sport's introduction in 1936 reportedly came as a result of Spain forfeiting the match after their players returned home to fight in their civil war.

"We went to Stockholm as British athletes; we came home Olympians, disciples of the leader, Coubertin, with a new vision I never lost."

Philip Noel-Baker, who competed for Great Britain in the 1,500m at Stockholm in 1912 and won silver in the event in Antwerp in 1920

The minimum diameter of Olympic medals is 6cm and they must be at least 3mm thick. The medal for first place must contain at least six grams of fine gold.

French President Jacques Chirac was accused by some of costing his country votes in the campaign to host the 2012 Games when, the day before the ballot, he said of Great Britain: "We can't trust people who have such bad food. After Finland, it's the country with the worst food."

Peter Markham Scott, who won a bronze medal for Great Britain in the monotype sailing class in 1936, was the son of the polar explorer Robert Falcon Scott.

The Olympic rings are intended to symbolise friendship between nations. The colours – blue, yellow, black, green and red on a white background – were selected because at least one of them appears on every national flag.

Jerzy Pawlowski was an Olympic hero for Poland,
winning five fencing medals and ending Hungary's
domination of the sabre event by winning gold in 1968.
But in the mid-1970s he was jailed for espionage, having
been exposed as a CIA agent. He served 10 years of
his 25-year sentence.

The first draw in the Olympic football final came in 1928,
with a 1–1 result between Uruguay and Argentina.
Uruguay won the replay 2–1.

Bermuda became the least populated nation to win a medal
at the Olympics when the boxer Clarence Hill won bronze in
the heavyweight division at Montreal in 1976. Bermuda had a
population of around 53,000 at the time.

Anita Lonsbrough of Great Britain in 1960 and Galina
Prozumenshchikova of the Soviet Union in 1964 were the only
competitors outside Australia and the United States to win a
gold medal in the swimming events.

Bobby Pearce reportedly paused his quarter-final effort
in the 1928 single sculls event to allow a family of ducks
to swim in front of his boat. With the ducks safe, the
Australian resumed and still won gold, repeating
his success in 1932.

Emil Rausch, who won freestyle gold medals at 880 yards and
at one mile in 1904, was reportedly the last swimmer to win
an event at the Games using the side stroke.

Great Britain's leading hurdler of the 1920s, David Cecil competed in three editions of the Games from 1924. As Lord Burghley, he became the first member of the House of Lords to win an Olympic athletics title when he won gold in 1928 in the 400m hurdles. In 1932 he added a silver in the 4x400m.

Horace Ashenfelter was an agent with the FBI in the United States. As he raced for the line to win gold in the 3,000m steeplechase in 1952, he was followed home – but not closely enough – by a Russian, Vladimir Kazantsev.

The distance of 26 miles and 385 yards for the marathon was set by chance when organisers of the 1908 Games in London decided the race should start from beneath the window of the royal nursery at Windsor Castle and conclude in front of the royal box at White City Stadium.

Olympic founder Baron Pierre de Coubertin was buried in Lausanne after his death in 1937 but his heart was buried separately in a monument near the ruins of ancient Olympia in Greece.

Race For The Line

1 *Johnny Douglas captained the England cricket team, including in an Ashes series victory in 1911. But in which Olympic sport did he win gold in 1908?*

2 *Who won a gold medal for literature under the pseudonyms Georges Hohrod and Martin Eschbach in the 1912 Olympic art competition for his poem "Ode To Sport"?*

3 *Which Scottish writer famed for detective stories was reporting on the 1908 Games for a newspaper when Dorando Pietri made his dramatic entrance to the stadium at the end of the marathon?*

4 *With the light fading as Bob Mathias won his first decathlon in 1948, how did the London officials reportedly illuminate the venue to allow the last two events to be completed?*

5 *Which of the home nations won the first Olympic hockey match with a 4–0 win over Germany when the sport made its debut at the 1908 Games?*

6 *Which sport did the 1968 Olympic 100m champion Jim Hines play professionally after his retirement from athletics?*

7 *A number of Olympic athletes have pursued acting careers after retiring, but which former actor officially opened the Games in 1984?*

8 *What did neighbours present to Fanny Blankers-Koen when she returned to the Netherlands after her gold medal successes in the 1948 Games?*

"I'm almost at a loss for words. To be the most decorated Olympian of all time, it just sounds weird."

Michael Phelps has the last word after taking his medal count to 16 – including 14 golds – at the 2008 Games in Beijing

9 *Which 1981 cinematic blend of fact and fiction was based on the story of Harold Abrahams and Eric Liddell at the 1924 Games in Paris?*

10 *Which form of hockey was included as a demonstration sport at the 1992 Games in Barcelona but has not appeared on the schedule since?*

11 *Which Scottish competitor won 200m breaststroke gold in 1976 to deny the United States a clean sweep of all 13 men's swimming medals?*

12 *At the Beijing Games what was the connection between Afghanistan, Togo, Tajikistan and Mauritius?*

Answers:

1 Boxing
2 Baron de Coubertin
3 Arthur Conan Doyle
4 They used car headlights
5 Scotland
6 American football
7 United States President Ronald Reagan
8 A bicycle
9 Chariots of Fire
10 Roller hockey
11 David Wilkie
12 They all won their first Olympic medal